KU-602-855

Tuscany & Florence

by Tim Jepson

Tim Jepson's love of travel began with a busking
trip through Europe, and since has taken him
from the Umbrian countryside to the Canadian
Rockies and the windswept tundra of the Yukon.
Tim has written many books for the AA, including
Explorer guides to *Canada*, *Rome*, *Italy*, *Florence
and Tuscany* and *Venice*. Other publications
include *Rough Guides* to *Tuscany and Canada*,
and *National Geographic Traveler* guides to *Italy
and Florence*.

Above: *The Campanile high above Florence*

AA Publishing

Written by Tim Jepson

First published 1998
Reprinted Nov 1998. Reprinted Nov 1999
Revised second edition 2000. Reprinted Aug 2001
Reprinted 2004. Information
verified and updated.
Reprinted May, Jul and Dec 2004
Reprinted Feb 2005
**Reprinted 2006. Information
verified and updated.**
Reprinted Apr 2006

*Peaceful Tuscan
landscape near
Monte Amiata*

© Automobile Association
Developments Limited 2004, 2006
Maps © Automobile Association
Developments Limited 2000, 2006

Published by AA Publishing, a trading name of Automobile
Association Developments Limited, whose registered office
is Fanum House, Basing View, Basingstoke, Hampshire
RG21 4EA. Registered number 1878835.

Find out more about
AA Publishing and the
wide range of travel
publications and services
the AA provides by
visiting our website at
www.theAA.com/
bookshop

A03045

Colour separation: Keenes, Andover
Printed and bound in Italy by Printer Trento S.r.l

Contents

About this Book

KEY TO SYMBOLS

➕ map reference to the maps found in the What to See section (see below)

✉ address or location

☎ telephone number

🕐 opening times

🍴 restaurant or café on premises or near by

Ⓜ nearest underground train station

🚌 nearest bus/tram route

🚆 nearest overground train station

⛴ ferry crossings and excursions by boat

✈ travel by air

ℹ tourist information

♿ facilities for visitors with disabilities

✋ admission charge

↔ other places of interest near by

❓ other practical information

➤ indicates the page where you will find a fuller description

This book is divided into five sections to cover the most important aspects of your visit to Tuscany and Florence.

Viewing Tuscany & Florence pages 5–14
An introduction to Tuscany and Florence by the author.
  Features of Tuscany and Florence
  Essence of Tuscany and Florence
  The Shaping of Tuscany and Florence
  Peace and Quiet
  Famous of Tuscany and Florence

Top Ten pages 15–26
The author's choice of the Top Ten places to see in Tuscany and Florence, each with practical information.

What to See pages 27–90
The main areas of Florence and Tuscany, each with its own brief introduction and an alphabetical listing of the main attractions.
  Practical information
  Snippets of "Did You Know…" information
  2 suggested walks
  2 suggested tours
  2 features

Where To… pages 91–116
Detailed listings of the best places to eat, stay, shop, take the children and be entertained.

4

Practical Matters pages 117–24
A highly visual section containing essential travel information.

Maps
All map references are to the individual maps found in the What to See section of this guide.
For example, Ponte Vecchio has the reference ➕ 28C2—indicating the page on which the map is located and the grid square in which the bridge is to be found. A list of all the maps that have been used in this travel guide can be found in the index.

Prices
Where appropriate, an indication of the cost of an establishment is given by € signs:
€€€ denotes higher prices, €€ denotes average prices, while € denotes lower charges.

Star Ratings
Most of the places described in this book have been given a separate rating:

✪✪✪   Do not miss
✪✪   Highly recommended
✪   Worth seeing

Viewing
Tuscany &
Florence

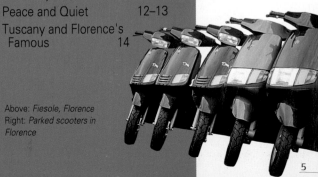

Above: *Fiesole, Florence*
Right: *Parked scooters in Florence*

Tim Jepson's Tuscany & Florence

Essential Florence
Baptistery: mosaics and doors
Campanile: general view
Cappella Brancacci: fresco cycle
Cappelle Medicee: Michelangelo sculptures
Duomo: view from the dome
Palazzo Medici-Riccardi: Gozzoli fresco cycle
Palazzo Pitti: paintings
Michelangelo's *David*
Santa Croce: tombs and frescoes
Santa Maria Novella: Masaccio's *Trinità* and fresco cycles
Uffizi: paintings

Essential Tuscany
Arezzo: San Francesco (frescoes of Piero della Francesca)
Cortona: Museo Diocesano (Fra Angelico paintings)
Lucca: Duomo, San Michele, walls and town
Monte Oliveto Maggiore: Sodoma and Signorelli frescoes
Pienza: Duomo, village
Pisa: Leaning Tower, Duomo and Baptistery
San Gimignano: Collegiata and village
Siena: Campo, Duomo, Ospedale, Museo dell'Opera, Pinacoteca e Palazzo Pubblico

Imagine you had to pick just one city to represent all that humankind has achieved. You would be hard pressed to improve on Florence, whose churches, museums and galleries contain some of the greatest works of art ever produced. Imagine, then, that you had to choose a landscape in which to live forever, one of whose beauty and endless variety you would never tire. You might happily plump for Tuscany, whose bucolic countryside has been fashioned by chance and centuries of toil into a glorious and almost perfect scenic patchwork.

Florence is not entirely devoted to art, however, and visitors who restrict themselves to paintings and sculpture will come away with memories of a forbidding indoor city. It's essential to leave the rather gloomy streets and brooding palaces for the city's gardens, bridges and half-hidden corners, and still more vital to join the Florentines—some of the most chic of all Italians—in their pursuit of outdoor pleasures, whether it's window-shopping in Via dei Tornabuoni or sipping drinks in the city's elegant, old-world cafés.

In Tuscany the choice of pleasure is greater still, from cities with a wide array of culture—notably Siena and Lucca—to the endless possibilities of the region's beautiful countryside. There are hills, mountains, sandy beaches, and a hundred village squares lined with rustic trattorias and bustling bars. And not so far from the beaten track lie towns such as Pienza, Cortona and San Gimignano, each a perfect combination of the culture, charm and beauty which make this unusually blessed region so irresistible.

An archetypal Tuscan landscape, complete with cypresses

Features of Tuscany & Florence

Geography
- Latitude of Florence: 43° 46 minutes north—the same as Toronto (Canada) and Sapporo (Japan)
- Longitude of Florence: 11° 14 minutes east
- Area of Tuscany: 22, 992sq km (8,875sq miles)
- Altitude of Florence: 49m(161ft) above sea level
- Height of Duomo: 91m (298ft)
- Highest point in Tuscany: Mt Cimone, 2,165m (7,101ft)
- Most densely wooded region in Italy: Tuscany
- Length of the River Arno in Tuscany: 241km (790ft)

Climate
- Average January temperature: 6°C (43°F)
- Average August temperature: 25°C (77°F)
- Average October rainfall: 12.4cm (5ins)
- Average July rainfall: 3.5cm (1.5ins)
- Average annual rainfall: 89.4cm (35ins)
- Height above street level of 1966 flood: 6m (19ft)

Degrees of Wealth
In the 15th century an average family could live comfortably on 150 florins a year (the florin was the standard Florentine currency). A palace could be bought for 1,000 florins, a Botticelli painting for 100, a slave for 50 and a servant for 10. To give some idea of the ruling Medici family's wealth, their account books for the years 1433–71 showed 663,755 florins spent over 38 years simply on 'buildings, charitie and taxes'.

People
- Population of Florence in June 1999: 403,294
- Population in June 1996: 381,762
- Population in June 1994: 388,969
- Population of Tuscany: 3.5 million

Crowds of visitors congregating on the Ponte Vecchio

Tourism
- Annual number of visitors to Florence: 7 million (estimate)
- Most popular museum and gallery: Galleria degli Uffizi
- Annual number of visitors to the Uffizi: about 1.5 million

Essence of Tuscany & Florence

Florence seduces with its art and culture, Tuscany with its hill-towns and timeless scenery. Europe's greatest Renaissance paintings and sculptures crowd the city's churches and galleries, while ancient vineyards, gnarled olives and cypress-topped hills make up one of Italy's most beautiful regional landscapes. Beyond the lures of culture and countryside, however, lie more subtle charms: the simple pleasures of a hazy-hilled view, for example; or the best ice creams and tastiest cappuccinos in Europe; bustling bars and pavement cafés; dining under the stars; or a stroll around geranium-hung streets on a summer evening.

THE **10** ESSENTIALS

*If you only have a short time to visit Tuscany &
Florence, or would like to get a really complete
picture of the region, here are the essentials:*

• **See Michelangelo's
David**—so familiar it's a
cliché, but something you
still have to see (▶ 19).
• **Climb the Campanile**—
struggle up the stairs for a
breathtaking view of
Florence (▶ 33).
Alternatively, climb to the
top of the cathedral dome for
a similar panorama (▶ 37).
• **See the top museums**—
you can't escape the art: Be
sure to visit the Uffizi for the
paintings (▶ 26)—reserve
ahead—and the Bargello for
the sculpture (▶ 22).

• **Take an evening stroll**—
head for the Arno bridges,
and the Ponte Vecchio in
particular, for some of
Florence's most romantic
nighttime views (▶ 52).
• **Sip a drink in the
Campo**—treat yourself to a
drink in a café on Siena's
Piazza del Campo, one of
Italy's most beautiful
medieval squares (▶ 16).
• **Enjoy an al fresco lunch**—
eating out is one of
Tuscany's greatest pleasures:
find a restaurant with outside
tables and forget the sight-

Above: *A peaceful
moment on the River
Arno at Pisa*

Left: *The Giardino di
Boboli are Italy's most
visited gardens (left)*

• **Walk in the Boboli
Gardens**—5 million visitors a
year can't be wrong: take a
break from sightseeing in
Italy's most visited gardens
(▶ 38).
• **Eat an ice cream**—buy an
ice cream from *Vivoli*, widely
considered to be one of
Italy's best *gelaterie*,
and eat it sitting in
nearby Piazza Santa
Croce (▶ 57).
• **Visit Santa
Croce**—Tuscany's
greats are buried in
this church, among
them Michelangelo,
Galileo and
Machiavelli. As an
added attraction
there are frescoes
by Giotto and other
medieval artists
(▶ 24).

seeing in favour of a leisurely
lunch (▶ 56 and 96–101).
• **Visit San Gimignano**—
busy in summer, but still the
village to see in Tuscany if
you see no other; known as
the 'medieval Manhattan'
after its ancient towers
(▶ 80–82).

Below: *Santa Croce rises
majestically above
Florence's rooftops*

The Shaping of Tuscany & Florence

An Etruscan plate, among Tuscany's earliest objects

800BC
First evidence of the Etruscans in Tuscany.

500BC
Etruscan expansion and the growth of an Etruscan colony at Fiesole in the hills above Florence.

205BC
The Romans establish control over Tuscany and exact tributes from the Etruscans.

59BC
Florence (*Florentia*) is founded as colony for retired army veterans, following laws promulgated by Julius Caesar.

20BC
Siena (*Saena*) is founded as a Roman military outpost.

AD250
Eastern monks and merchants bring Christianity to Florence.

552
Totila the Goth and a barbarian army attack Florence.

570
The Lombards conquer much of northern Italy and establish a base in Lucca.

800
Charlemagne defeats the Lombards and is crowned Holy Roman Emperor. Tuscany is ruled from Lucca by imperial princes known as Margraves.

1115
Matilda, the last Margrave, bequeaths her territories to the papacy with the exception of Lucca, Florence and Siena.

1125
Florence defeats and absorbs Fiesole.

1186
Work begins on Siena cathedral.

1215
Conflicts between the papacy and Holy Roman Empire (Guelphs and Ghibellines) favour the development of independent city states.

1252
Florence prospers through her textile trade and mints the first gold florin (*fiorino*): merchant guilds achieve wealth and power.

1260
Siena defeats Florence at the Battle of Montaperti.

1302
Dante is exiled from Florence and begins writing *The Divine Comedy*.

1348
The Black Death ravages Tuscany and leads to economic collapse.

1350
The Leaning Tower of Pisa is completed.

1360
Birth of Giovanni di Bicci de' Medici, founder of the Medici banking empire.

1389
Birth of Cosimo de' Medici, greatest member of the Medici dynasty.

1402
Competition held to design Florence's Baptistery doors.

1406
Florence defeats Pisa and gains access to the sea.

1436
Brunelleschi finishes work on Florence's cathedral dome.

1469
Birth of Machiavelli and the accession of Lorenzo de' Medici, or Lorenzo the Magnificent.

1475
Birth of Michelangelo: Donatello sculpts *David*.

1485
Botticelli paints *The Birth of Venus*.

1494
Florence surrenders to Charles VIII of France: Savonarola, a zealous monk, seizes control of the city.

Cosimo I, Florence's 16th-century Medici ruler

1498
Savonarola is burned at the stake for heresy and Florence briefly becomes a republic.

1504
Michelangelo sculpts the statue of *David*.

1512
Combined papal and Spanish armies defeat Florence and return the Medici to power.

1537
Cosimo I, a Medici, rules Florence as a Spanish and Austrian puppet.

1570
Cosimo proves his own man and founds the Grand Duchy of Tuscany.

1743
The death of the last Medici sees Florence and the Grand Duchy pass eventually to Austrian control.

1799
Napoleon defeats Austria and occupies Florence.

1815
Following Napoleon's defeat most of Tuscany is returned by treaty to the Austrians.

1860
The Austrians are defeated and Tuscany joins a united Italy.

1865
Florence is capital of a united Italy until 1871, when Rome is freed from French and papal rule.

1944
Florentine and Tuscan towns and art treasures are damaged by Allied bombing and the retreating Nazis.

1966
Florence is ravaged by floods after the Arno bursts its banks.

1993
A terrorist bomb damages part of the Uffizi.

1996
Florence hosts the G7 economic summit.

2001
The Leaning Tower of Pisa reopens to the public after 11 years.

Peace & Quiet

Alpi Apuane

The Apuan Alps contain Tuscany's most spectacular scenery, forming a jagged crest of mountains above the Versilian coast north of Pisa and Lucca. Marble mines streak their western flanks, the source for centuries of stone which has served sculptors from Michelangelo to Henry Moore. On their eastern borders, chestnut-covered slopes fall away to the Garfagnana, a dulcet valley by the pleasant little towns of Barga and Caselnuovo (Barga, in particular, is well worth visiting for its lovely cathedral). Well-marked trails criss cross the slopes, wending through woods or cresting the panoramic and craggy summit ridges. Excellent walking maps of the region are widely available, making it easy to undertake light strolls or proper hikes. Stazzema and Levigliani make good departure points in the west; late May is the best time to see the area's renowned spring flowers. Driving is also a delight, the excellent folk museum in San Pellegrino in Alpe (16km/10 miles northeast of Castelnuovo) being a particularly good target. The mountains have protected park status, and are earmarked for future national park designation.

Chianti

Tuscany's most famous scenic enclave is a region of rambling wooded hills, sunflower-filled fields and vine-covered slopes between Florence and Siena. It is a pretty rather than spectacularly beautiful region, best suited to leisurely exploration by car (➤ 79), bicycle or—given its ever-improving maps—on foot. It is also a surprisingly

The rolling hills and vineyards of Chianti make up one of Tuscany's loveliest landscapes

The spectacular mountains of the Alpi Apuane provide excellent walking country

empty area, its wooded mantle broken only by the occasional farmhouse and small town. Places such as Radda, Gaiole and Castellina are slightly disappointing, often spoilt by new building and a sprawl of light industry, but they are good places to sample Chianti's famous wines. The region is also liberally scattered with remote vineyards, where you can buy directly from local producers: follow one of the many 'wine roads' or look out for the well-signposted *cantine* offering *vendita diretta* (direct sales). Tramping lonely paths or driving gravel roads (*strade bianche*) offer the chance of wildlife sightings: crested porcupines, deer and wild boar, among other creatures, all make the Chianti hills their home.

Monte Amiata

Tuscany's fringes are filled with outstanding areas of natural beauty: the Maremma on the coast, for example, or the forests of the Casentino in the east and the meadow-topped hills of the Pratomagno, above Arezzo. All these are some way from the region's key towns, however, while Monte Amiata, easily reached from Siena, is one of the area's more convenient scenic retreats. A forested mountain of volcanic origin, its looming profile dominates much of southern Tuscany. Tiny villages cling to its far-flung slopes—Arcidosso, Santa Fiora, Piancastagnaio—all worth a few minutes' attention if you are exploring by car. A road reaches virtually to the summit (1,738m/5,700ft), a popular spot, complete with bars and restaurants, where vast views unfold as far as the sea. Quieter retreats await in the woods below, where you can follow any number of marked trails or find a quiet corner to yourself.

Famous of Tuscany & Florence

Dante, great medieval poet and author of The Divine Comedy

Dante

Dante was born in 1265 into a minor noble family. Educated in Bologna and Padua, he became a civic official and diplomat, eventually joining Florence's ruling Priorate in 1300. He joined a Guelph faction which fell from grace, a change of fortune which led to his forced exile in 1302. Bitterly rejecting his native city, he moved around Italy, eventually settling in Ravenna. There he probably wrote most of *The Divine Comedy*, an epic poem partly inspired by his doomed love for Beatrice, whom he first met when he was nine and she was eight. He died in 1321 and is buried in Ravenna.

Galileo

Born in Pisa in 1564, the son of a musician, Galileo Galilei moved to Florence in 1574. He was educated in medicine at Pisa and eventually took up a teaching post in the city; while there he dropped weights from the Leaning Tower to disprove Aristotle's assertion that bodies of different masses fall at different speeds. Later his development of powerful telescopes enabled him to make key discoveries in the field of astronomy. However, his heretical assertion that the earth was not the central focal point of the heavens led to persecution by the Inquisition. Though saved by his friendship with Pope Urban VII, he remained under house arrest in Florence, where he continued to work until his death in 1642.

Machiavelli

Niccolò Machiavelli was born in Florence in 1469 into an impoverished noble family. 'I learnt to do without', he wrote, 'before I learnt to enjoy'. After entering politics in 1498 he became chancellor and secretary to the war council of the Florentine republic. He spent periods in France, Switzerland and Germany, sojourns which enabled him to view first hand the machinations of powerful political figures. Following the return of the Medici in 1512 he fell from grace, retiring to write *Il Principe (The Prince)*, a book which brilliantly united political science with the study of human nature. Later he was employed as an advisor to Giuliano de' Medici. He died in 1527.

Girolamo Savonarola

Born in 1452, Savonarola ran away to a Bologna monastery at 23, later moving to San Marco in Florence. By 1491 his apocalyptic sermons were drawing crowds of 10,000 to the Duomo. When Charles VII entered Italy in 1494 causing the Medici to flee, the monk became the city's effective ruler. In 1497 he was excommunicated for criticising Alexander VI, the corrupt Borgia pope, and a year later the Florentines turned against him. He was burned to death in Piazza della Signoria, where a plaque still marks the site of his execution.

Top Ten

Above: *Pisa's Leaning Tower*
Right: *Michelangelo's* David

1
Campo, Piazza del

Siena's magnificent central piazza and its arc of rosy palaces make up one of Europe's most beautiful medieval squares.

An arc of palaces and airy open spaces make the Campo one of Europe's loveliest medieval squares

✚ 87C2

✉ Piazza del Campo, Siena

☎ None

🕐 Daily 24 hours

🍽 Many cafés (€–€€) and restaurants (€€€)

🚌 In the pedestrian zone

♿ Good, but sloping and uneven paving

✋ Free

↔ Duomo (➤ 20), Palazzo Pubblico (➤ 87)

Walking into the Campo from Siena's tight huddle of streets is like stepping on to some medieval stage set. Situated at the heart of the old city, the conch-shaped piazza resembles a vast amphitheatre, its broad sweep of palaces culminating in the battlemented grandeur of the Palazzo Pubblico and its attendant bell tower.

The square probably began life as the Roman forum, becoming the town's principal marketplace before taking on its present form in 1293, when the Council of Nine, Siena's governing body, began to buy up land with a view to creating a great central square. The carefully chosen area was at the heart of Siena's *terzi* (the city's three main districts), and was the only piece of land owned by none of Siena's *contrade*, the city's fiercely competitive medieval parishes. As such the Council hoped the square would become the focus of civic life, a physical expression of good government, and a symbol of citizens' loyalty to Siena rather than to factions, families, *terzi* or *contrade*.

The Campo was completed in 1349 with the addition of its brick paving, whose nine sections were designed to symbolize the Council of Nine, and the folds of the Virgin's cloak, sheltering the city under its protective embrace. Both the Palazzo Pubblico and Torre del Mangia are well worth visiting, but you should also indulge in at least one pricey cappuccino at one of the Campo's cafés, an ideal way to take in the square's endless street life. Be warned, however, most of the restaurants are very expensive.

2
Cappelle Medicee

The Medici's private chapels and mausoleum feature several of Michelangelo's most outstanding pieces of Florentine funerary sculpture.

The Medici Chapels consist of the Crypt, a mausoleum for minor members of the Medici; the Cappella dei Principi, a vast and opulent chapel dedicated to six of the Medici Grand Dukes; and the Sagrestia Nuova, the last resting place of four of the family's leading lights.

The Crypt is the least interesting area, its dour, low-ceilinged vaults dotted with the brass-railed tombs of 49 lesser Medici. All were buried pell-mell in 1791 by Ferdinand III, only to be exhumed and re-buried in a more dignified manner in 1857. Steps lead from here to the Cappella dei Principi, begun as a family mausoleum for Cosimo I in 1604. A riot of decoration, this vast, marble-lined chapel was the most expensive project ever commissioned by the Medici. Around the walls, 16 coats of arms represent Medici-controlled Tuscan towns.

A corridor leads to the Sagrestia Nuova (New Sacristy), designed as a contrast to Brunelleschi's Old Sacristy in nearby San Lorenzo. It contains three groups of sculpture (1520–34), two wholly and one partly by Michelangelo. On the left is the tomb of Lorenzo, grandson of Lorenzo the Magnificent, whose statue symbolizes the contemplative life. On the right stands the tomb of Giuliano, third son of Lorenzo the Magnificent, symbolizing the active life. The third (unfinished) group—a Madonna and Child—was intended as the tomb of Lorenzo the Magnificent and his brother Giuliano.

28C5

Piazza Madonna degli Aldobrandini, Florence

055/238 8602; advance reservation 055/294 883

Tue–Sun 8.15–4.45 (also 2nd and 4th Mon of month). Closed 2nd and 4th Sun of month

Nearby (€)

In the pedestrian zone: nearest service 1, 6, 7

Few

Expensive

Battistero (▶ 32), Campanile (▶ 33), Duomo (▶ 36–7), San Lorenzo (▶ 54–5), Santa Maria Novella (▶ 58–9)

Visit in conjunction with San Lorenzo (▶ 54–5)

Admiring Michelangelo's sculptures in the Cappelle Medicee

3
Collegiata di San Gimignano

64C4

Piazza del Duomo 1, San Gimignano

0577/940 316

Church and Cappella di Santa Fina: Apr–end Oct Mon–Fri 9.30–7.10, Sat 9.30–5.10, Sun 12.30–5.10; Mar, Nov Mon–Sat 9.30–4.30, Sun 10.30–4.30; Dec–Feb closed except for servies. Check with tourist office

Nearby in Piazza della Cisterna (€–€€)

In the pedestrian zone

Few   Moderate

Museo Civico, Piazza della Cisterna, Torre Grossa, Sant'Agostino (▶81–2)

A series of superbly preserved medieval frescoes almost completely covers the Collegiata, San Gimignano's most important church.

Most people visit the beautiful village of San Gimignano for its 13 famous medieval towers (▶80–82), only to find that the most memorable part of their visit is the fresco-covered Collegiata, a church which served as the village's cathedral until San Gimignano ceased to be a bishopric. Begun in 1148, but later enlarged, it has little in its simple Romanesque façade to prepare you for the decorative wonder inside. Tuscany is filled with fresco cycles, and those in the Collegiata are not necessarily the region's most famous, but few cycles are as extensive, and few have the charm of these lovely paintings. The first panels, by Taddeo di Bartolo, fill the church's back wall and depict the Last Judgement (1393), with Paradise and Hell portrayed on two adjoining walls. Below is a large St. Sebastian by Benozzo Gozzoli (1420–97), a pupil of Fra Angelico, well-known for his depictions of contemporary life and pageantry (▶47).

On the church's right-hand (south) wall is a 22-panel cycle attributed to Lippo Memmi, a 14th-century Sienese artist, which depicts various New Testament scenes from the Passion and the Life of Christ. On the opposite wall are 26 panels (1367) by Bartolo di Fredi, a cycle of Old Testament episodes including scenes from the stories of Genesis, Abraham, Joseph, Moses and Job. To the left of the high altar, the Cappella di San Gimignano has a fine altar (1475) by Benedetto da Maiano, the sculptor who was responsible for the altar, marble shrine and bas-reliefs in the Cappella di Santa Fina (top of the right aisle). This chapel, however,

San Gimignano's churches and courtyards are beautifully decorated with medieval frescoes

is better known for its fresco cycle by Domenico Ghirlandaio (1449–94), another artist whose work reflects the tone and life of his own period. This cycle depicts the Life of St. Fina, one of San Gimignano's patron saints. Look out for the fresco which features a 15th-century view of the town.

4
David

Michelangelo's celebrated statue is one of the most familiar of all Renaissance images, and one of the essential sights of any visit to Florence.

Michelangelo's *David* is exhibited in the Galleria dell'Accademia, Europe's first artistic academy (founded in 1563), together with five other Michelangelo statues and an interesting collection of Gothic and Renaissance paintings. Italy's most famous sculpture was commissioned by the Opera del Duomo in 1501 when Michelangelo was just 26. Its theme—David defeating the tyrant Goliath—was chosen to symbolize the virtues of Florence (then a republic), its freedom from papal and foreign domination, and its recent liberation from Savonarola and the Medici. The marble from which it was sculpted, a vast 5-m (16-ft) block, had been quarried from Carrara some 40 years earlier but was so thin and riddled with cracks that it had defied the ambitions of all other sculptors. In Michelangelo's hands however, it was transformed in just three years into a work that secured his reputation as the foremost sculptor of his day.

When it was completed 30 leading artists were asked to select a site for the statue. The Piazza della Signoria was their eventual choice. There *David* remained, ravaged by wind and rain, until 1873. The fact that the figure was intended as a piece of outdoor sculpture helps to explain its famous distortions—notably the over-large hands and face—features designed to emphasise its monumentality.

Elsewhere in the gallery are Michelangelo's *St. Matthew* (1504–8) and four unfinished *Slaves*, or *Prisoners* (1521–3), the latter a graphic illustration of Michelangelo's dictum that sculpture was the liberation of a form which was already 'imprisoned' in the stone. There are also paintings by such masters as Botticelli, Perugino, Pontormo, Filippino Lippi and others.

✝ 29E5

✉ Via Ricasoli 60, Florence

☎ 055/238 8609; advance reservation 055/294 883

🕐 Tue–Sun 8.15–6.50

🍽 Nearby in Piazza San Marco and Via del Ricasoli (€)

🚌 1, 6, 7, 11 and other services to San Marco

♿ Good

✋ Expensive

↔ Museo di San Marco (➤ 23), Santissima Annunziata (➤ 53)

Michelangelo's David is one of the supreme works of the Renaissance

5
Duomo di Siena

🕂 86B2

✉ Piazza del Duomo, Siena

☎ 0577/283 048

🕐 Duomo: Mar–end Oct
Mon–Sat 7.30–7.30,
Sun 2–7.30; Nov–end
Feb Mon–Sat 7.30–5,
Sun 2–6.30
Libreria Piccolomini:
Mar–end Oct Mon–Sat
10.30–7.30, Sun
1.30–6.30; Nov–end Feb
Mon–Sat 10.30–6.30,
Sun 1.30–5.30
Baptistery: mid-Mar to
end Sep daily 9–7.30;
Oct 9–6; Nov to mid-
Mar 10–1, 2–5

🍴 Nearby (€)

🚌 In the pedestrian zone:
occasional shuttle bus
services

♿ None: several steps to
main entrance

✋ Duomo: free. Libreria
and Baptistery:
inexpensive

↔ Campo (▶ 16), Museo
dell'Opera del Duomo
(▶ 85), Ospedale di
Santa Maria della Scala
(▶ 86), Palazzo
Pubblico (▶ 87),
Pinacoteca Nazionale
(▶ 88)

❓ Two combined tickets
available: one for
Libreria, Baptistery and
Museo dell'Opera; other
for these sights plus
Museo Diocesano,
Sant'Agostino and
Oratorio di San
Bernardino

*The dazzling façade of
Siena's cathedral is a
masterpiece of
Romanesque and Gothic
architecture*

20

*This magnificent Gothic cathedral boasts one of
Italy's loveliest façades and an interior bursting
with a variety of outstanding works of art.*

Siena's cathedral was begun in 1196 and completed in
1376, during which time there was an aborted attempt to
extend the building, a scheme whose half-finished results
can be seen in the skeletal shell to the right of the present
structure. Much of the lower part of the façade (1285) was
designed by Giovanni Pisano, though most of his original
statuary is now in the nearby Museo dell'Opera.

The exterior's distinctive black-and-white banding is
echoed in the interior's monochrome pavement, which
consists of 56 panels (1349–1547) created over the
centuries by some of Siena's leading artists. Midway down
the left aisle (fourth altar) stands the Piccolomini altar,
whose four lower-niche statues are early works by
Michelangelo. Alongside lies the entrance to the Libreria
Piccolomini, beautifully frescoed by Pinturicchio with
scenes from the life of Aeneas Piccolomini (1509), a
Tuscan nobleman who became Pope Pius II.

At the end of the left aisle stands the Duomo's masterpiece: Nicola Pisano's Gothic pulpit (1268). To its left, in
the corner chapel, is Tino da Camaino's influential Tomb of
Cardinal Petroni (1318). Below it lies Donatello's bronze
pavement Tomb of Bishop Pecci (1426). The circular
Cappella di San Giovanni in the left transept has a bronze
statue of John the Baptist by Donatello and more
Pinturicchio frescoes. A similar chapel in the opposite
transept, the Cappella Chigi, was designed by Bernini. To
the rear of the cathedral be sure to visit the Baptistery,
which features swathes of lovely 15th-century frescoes
and a font with bronze panels by Ghiberti, Donatello and
Jacopo della Quercia.

6
Museo Nazionale del Bargello

✚ 29E3

✉ Via del Proconsolo 4, Florence

Italy's greatest collection of Renaissance sculpture is contained in the Bargello, together with an array of majolica, tapestries, paintings and silverware.

☎ 055/238 8606; advance reservation 055/294 883

🕐 Tue–Sun 8.15–1.50

🍴 Nearby in Via del Proconsolo (€)

🚌 19

♿ Good: lift to upper floor

✋ Moderate

↔ Museo di Firenze com'era (▶ 40), Palazzo Vecchio (▶ 50), Piazza della Signoria (▶ 51)

The fortress-like Bargello, begun in 1255, was Florence's earliest civic palace, serving first as the city's seat of government and later as the home of the chief of police. Later still it became a prison, torture chamber and place of execution, assuming its present role in 1865. The museum spreads over three floors, though its key works are found in just two large rooms. The first lies to the right of the ticket hall, and concentrates on the late Renaissance works of Michelangelo, Giambologna and Benvenuto Cellini. Michelangelo is represented by three contrasting works: a delicate tondo of the Madonna and Child; a powerful portrait bust of Brutus; and a lurching, soft-bellied statue of Bacchus. Other highlights include a bronze of Cosimo I by Cellini and Giambologna's celebrated Mercury, a sublime study in speed.

From this first room, wander into the courtyard, glance at the exterior sculptures in the small rooms opposite, and then climb the external staircase to the first floor. At the top of the stairs is a wonderful menagerie of bronze animals by Giambologna. Turn right and you come to the museum's second major room, a glorious vaulted hall filled with sculptural masterpieces. Look in particular for the works of Donatello, notably his St. George, removed from Orsanmichele; the Marzocco, Florence's heraldic lion; and the debonair and famously androgynous statue of David. Subsequent rooms are crammed with all manner of interesting rugs, tapestries, glassware, silverware and many other precious objets d'art. Particularly noteworthy is the Salone del Camino, which contains Italy's most important collection of small bronzes.

A delicate marble frieze by Francesco Rustici, one of many masterpieces in the Bargello

7
Museo di San Marco

The ancient Dominican convent of San Marco is renowned for a series of sublime frescoes and paintings by Fra Angelico.

San Marco was originally owned by Vallombrosan and Sylvestrine monks, passing to the Dominicans in 1436, when it was restored at Cosimo de' Medici's personal expense. Its subsequent priors included Fra Angelico, not only a devout Dominican, but also one of the finest of Florence's early Renaissance painters. Today the convent buildings are a museum given over almost entirely to the artist's paintings and frescoes.

Many of the paintings are contained in the Ospizio dei Pellegrini, a room once used to provide pilgrims with food and shelter (located off the main cloister). Its two masterpieces hang on opposite walls: a Deposition (1440), removed from the church of Santa Trínita, and the Madonna dei Linaiuoli (1433), commissioned for the headquarters of the flax-makers' (*linaiuoli*) guild. Also off the cloister is the Sala Capitolare, or Chapter House, which features a Crucifixion (1442) by Fra Angelico. The Refectory nearby contains a large fresco of the Last Supper by Domenico Ghirlandaio (beyond the shop).

Steps from the cloister lead to the first floor, where you are greeted by Fra Angelico's famous

✚	29E6
✉	Piazza San Marco, Florence
☎	055/238 8608; advance reservations 055/294 883
🕐	Mon–Fri 8.15/30–1.50, Sat 8.15/30–6.50, Sun 8.15/30–7. Closed 1st, 3rd, 5th Sun and 2nd, 4th Mon of month
🍴	Nearby in Piazza San Marco (€)
🚌	1, 6, 7, 10, 11, 17, 20, 25, 31, 32, 33
♿	Good ✋ Moderate
↔	*David*, Galleria dell'Accademia (➤ 19), Palazzo Medici-Riccardi (➤ 47)

Annunciation (c.1445), one of the most beautiful of all Renaissance paintings. The rest of the floor is largely taken up by 44 dormitory cells, each frescoed by Fra Angelico and his pupils with religious scenes intended as aids to monastic devotion. At the end of the far corridor are three cells once occupied by Savonarola. At the end of the corridor on your right are two cells, larger than the rest, once used by Cosimo il Vecchio de' Medici. Close by is Europe's first public library, designed for Cosimo by Michelozzo in 1441.

The San Marco museum contains numerous paintings by Fra Angelico and other Renaissance artists

23

8
Santa Croce

29F2

Piazza Santa Croce, Florence

055/246 6105

Mon–Sat 9–5.30, Sun 1–5.30; may open later in summer

Nearby in Piazza Santa Croce (€)

13, 23, shuttle bus B

Good

Church: moderate; includes Museo dell'Opera di Santa Croce and Cappella dei Pazzi

Museo Nazionale del Bargello (➤ 22), Museo Bardini (➤ 40)

The most famous church in Florence is celebrated for its superb Giotto frescoes and the tombs of Galileo, Michelangelo and Machiavelli.

Begun in 1294 by Arnolfo di Cambio, and completed in 1450, this Franciscan foundation attracted the attention of many wealthy families, all anxious to seek spiritual salvation by being buried among the 'humble' Franciscans; hence the many tombs and the various frescoed family chapels (notably those of the Bardi, Peruzzi and Baroncelli).

Among those buried in the church are Michelangelo (first tomb on the right), Machiavelli (sixth on the right) and Galileo (first on the left). There are also outstanding examples of Renaissance funerary sculpture, notably 15th-century works by Bernardo Rossellino (end of the right aisle) and Desiderio da Settignano (end of the left aisle). More famous still are the church's fresco cycles, the best known of which are by Giotto, who was responsible for the paintings in the Cappella Bardi and the Cappella Peruzzi (adjacent chapels to the right of the high altar).

To the right of the church lie the Cappella dei Pazzi (1430) and the Museo dell'Opera di Santa Croce. The former, rather austere chapel by Brunelleschi, is simply decorated with 12 terracotta tondi of the Apostles by Luca della Robbia, who also decorated the portico and polychrome roundels in the upper corners (attributed to Brunelleschi and Donatello). The Museo's highlights are Donatello's St. Louise of Toulouse and a crucifix by Cimabue.

9
Torre Pendente
(Leaning Tower)

Few sights are as immediately recognizable as the Leaning Tower of Pisa, one of several monuments in Pisa's beautiful Campo dei Miracoli.

Pisa's famous Leaning Tower was begun in 1173 as a companion piece for the city's Duomo and Baptistery, two buildings which make up a lovely medieval ensemble in a green-lawned square known as the Campo dei Miracoli (the 'Field of Miracles'). The tower began to lean almost from the outset, tilting into the sandy subsoil under the foundations (this part of the coast was once under water, so that local soil is composed almost entirely of sand and silt). Initial construction work on the tower was abandoned after only three storeys were complete, but work resumed in the 13th century when it was accepted that the tower would not fall. Over the next 180 years a series of architects tried to correct the lean by adding off-centre sections. None was successful. At its worst, the tower was a dizzying 5.2m (17ft) to the vertical.

Architects long agonized over how to prevent the tower's collapse and reverse the lean. Numerous schemes were put forward and half-heartedly considered, but none was taken seriously until the tower was closed to the public in 1990 after it was deemed to have become dangerous. Over the next few years, some 900 tonnes of lead were strapped to the tower's base on its northern side to help counter the lean. By 1998 some improvement had been seen, and a delicate drilling operation began to remove water and subsoil from the tower's northern foundations. The drying of the soil and the removal of material, created a gradual subsidence on one side of the tower, which saw the lean corrected by around 10 per cent, bringing it to the angle it had in 1838. The project cost over £20 million and took 11 years to complete—the site was officially reopened in November 2001.

🕂 64B5

✉ Campo (Piazza) dei Miracoli, Pisa

☎ Tours must be prebooked (050/506 547/www.opapisa.it)

🕐 Tours only every 35–40 mins: Apr–end Sep daily 8.30–8.30; Mar, Oct 8.30–7.30; Nov–end Feb 9.30–5. Late opening mid-Jun–end Sep; call to confirm

🍴 Nearby (€)

🚌 1 from rail station

♿ Campo dei Miracoli: good

✋ Campo dei Miracoli: free

The Leaning Tower began to tilt almost from the moment it was built in 1173

25

10
Uffizi, Galleria degli

29D2

Loggiato degli Uffizi 6, off Piazza della Signoria, Florence

055/238 8651

Tue–Sun 8.15–6.50. Closed Mon, 1 Jan, Easter Sun, 1 May, 15 Aug, 25 Dec

Café (€)

In the pedestrian zone

Good

Expensive

Museo di Storia della Scienza (➤ 45), Orsanmichele (➤ 46), Palazzo Vecchio (➤ 50), Piazza della Signoria (➤ 51), Ponte Vecchio (➤ 52)

Tickets can be reserved for admission at a set time to the Uffizi and other museums by calling Firenze Musei 055/294 883

A Madonna by Filippo Lippi, one of the Uffizi's countless masterpieces

One of the world's finest art galleries, the Uffizi contains a collection of paintings that features all the great names of the Florentine Renaissance.

The building housing the Uffizi was begun by Vasari in 1560, its original purpose being to serve as a suite of offices (*uffizi*) from which the Medici could administer the Grand Duchy of Tuscany. In 1737 it was bequeathed to Florence, along with the Medici art collection, by Anna Luisa, sister of Gian Gastone, the last Medici Grand Duke. Today its 45 rooms house not only the cream of 14th- and 15th-century Florentine paintings, but also masterpieces from elsewhere in Italy (notably Venice and Siena), together with a surprising number of major works from Germany, Holland and Spain. Rooms 1–15 are given over to the Florentine Renaissance (and contain the most famous paintings); rooms 16–27 concentrate on the age of High Renaissance and Mannerism, and rooms 28–45 are devoted to later Italian and European paintings.

Highlights are too numerous to mention, though certain works deserve extra special attention. Room 2 opens with altarpieces of the *Maestà* (*Madonna Enthroned*) by Giotto, Duccio and Cimabue, three of Italy's greatest 13th-century painters, who contributed to the movement towards naturalism and emotion and away from the stilted and more stylized Byzantine approach to subjects in art. Room 3's Sienese paintings are dominated by Simone Martini's sublime *Annunciation*, while in rooms 5 and 6 the key work is Gentile da Fabriano's exquisitely detailed *Adoration of the Magi*. Rooms 10–14 feature paintings by Botticelli, notably the famous *Primavera* and *Birth of Venus*. Room 18 is best known for the *Venus de' Medici*, renowned for centuries as one of antiquity's most erotic statues. Successive rooms feature works by, among others, Raphael, Caravaggio and Michelangelo; the Venetians Titian, Giorgione and Carpaccio; and Europeans such as Rembrandt, Rubens and Van Dyck.

What
To See

Above: *Pisa*
Right: *Baptistery door, Florence*

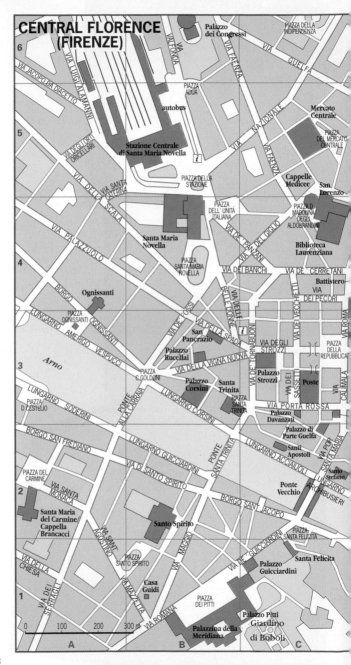

CENTRAL FLORENCE (FIRENZE)

Palazzo dei Congressi

PIAZZA DELLA INDIPENDENZA

VIA VALFONDA

VIA FAENZA

VIA GUELFA

VIA LUIGI ALAMANNI

VIA JACOPO DA DIACETO

PIAZZA ADUA

autobus

Mercato Centrale

VIA NAZIONALE

VIA FAENZA

PIAZZA DEL MERCATO CENTRALE

VIA DEGLI ORTI ORICELLARI

Stazione Centrale di Santa Maria Novella

PIAZZA DELLA STAZIONE

i

Cappelle Medicee

San Lorenzo

VIA DELLA SCALA

VIA SANTA CATERINA

PIAZZA DELL' UNITÀ ITALIANA

PIAZZA D. MADONNA DEGLI ALDOBRANDINI

Biblioteca Laurenziana

VIA PALAZZUOLO

Santa Maria Novella

VIA DE' PANZANI

VIA DEL GIGLIO

PIAZZA SANTA MARIA NOVELLA

VIA DEI BANCHI

VIA DE' CERRETANI

Battistero

VIA DEI PECORI

BORGO

Ognissanti

VIA DELLE BELLE DONNE

VIA DELLE

VIA DE' VECCHIETTI

VIA ROMA

PIAZZA OGNISSANTI

LUNGARNO AMERIGO VESPUCCI

OGNISSANTI

VIA DE' FOSSI

VIA DELLA VIGNA NUOVA

San Pancrazio

i

VIA DE' TORNABUONI

VIA DEGLI STROZZI

PIAZZA DELLA REPUBBLICA

Arno

Palazzo Rucellai

VIA DELLA SPADA

Palazzo Strozzi

VIA DEI SASSETTI

Poste

VIA CALIMALA

LUNGARNO SODERINI

PIAZZA D'CESTELIO

PIAZZA C. GOLDONI

Palazzo Corsini

Santa Trinita

PIAZZA SANTA TRINITA

VIA PORTA ROSSA

PONTE ALLA CARRAIA

LUNGARNO CORSINI

Palazzo Davanzati

Palazzo di Parte Guelfa

BORGO SAN FREDIANO

LUNGARNO GUICCIARDINI

PONTE SANTA TRINITA

LUNGARNO ACCIAIUOLI

Santi Apostoli

VIA POR S. MARIA

VIA DI SANTO SPIRITO

Ponte Vecchio

Santo Stefano

LUNGARNO ARCHIBUSIERI

PIAZZA DEL CARMINE

VIA SANTA MONACA

BORGO SANT' JACOPO

Santa Maria del Carmine / Cappella Brancacci

VIA SANT' AGOSTINO

Santo Spirito

VIA MAGGIO

PIAZZA SANTA FELICITA

VIA DELLA CHIESA

PIAZZA SANTO SPIRITO

VIA DE' GUICCIARDINI

Santa Felicita

Palazzo Guicciardini

VIA DEI SERRAGLI

Casa Guidi

VIA MAZZETTA

PIAZZA DEI PITTI

Palazzo Pitti

VIA ROMANA

Palazzina della Meridiana

Giardino di Boboli

0   100   200   300 m

6   5   4   3   2   1

A   B   C

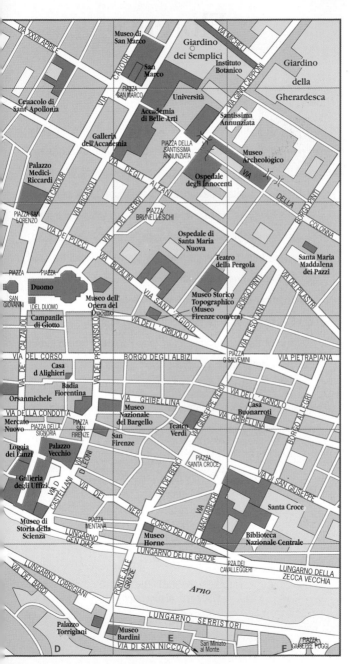

Florence

Florence is a city-sized shrine to the Renaissance, its streets filled with churches and monuments, its galleries overflowing with some of Europe's greatest paintings and sculptures. Five centuries ago the city was almost without equal, its artistic and intellectual ferment unparalleled, its wealth virtually unsurpassed. Patronage from families such as the Medici provided the spur for innovation, creating an atmosphere in which creativity and individual genius flourished as never before.

Yet Florence today is far more than a vast museum. The Giardino di Boboli provides open green space, bustling street markets offer a taste of vibrant life, and tiny back alleys hide intimate medieval nooks and artisans' workshops. Tree-lined squares conceal sunny cafés, while restaurants and ice-cream parlours abound, as alluring as any painting or sculpture.

'...Beautiful
The city lies along the
ample vale,
Cathedral, tower and palace,
piazza and street,
The river trailing like a
silver cord...'

ELIZABETH BARRETT BROWNING
(1806–61), *Aurora Leigh*

Florence

Florence is compact and easily explored on foot, though its wealth of art and culture, and the way sights are scattered across the city, means it is difficult to plan convenient sightseeing itineraries. The historic heart conforms to the grid of the old Roman colony, its principal points of interest lying on and around two main squares: Piazza del Duomo and Piazza della Signoria.

Most people begin a tour of the city in Piazza del Duomo, where you should see the Duomo (cathedral), Baptistery and Museo dell'Opera, as well as climb the Campanile or cathedral dome for a superb view of the city. Close by lies the Museo Nazionale del Bargello, Italy's greatest collection of Renaissance sculpture. Via dei Calzaiuoli, Florence's pedestrianized main street, leads south to Piazza della Signoria, where you should visit the Palazzo Vecchio, the Uffizi—Italy's most famous art gallery—and the nearby Museo di Storia della Scienza.

North of the central district the key sights are the Cappelle Medicee, with statues by Michelangelo, the Accademia (home to Michelangelo's *David*) and the Palazzo Medici-Riccardi, with its lovely fresco cycle. A little further north lies the Museo di San Marco, filled with sublime paintings by Fra Angelico. The city's two most important churches—Santa Croce and Santa Maria Novella—lie east and west of the centre respectively. Across the Arno, the river that divides the city, is the quieter Oltrarno district, worth visiting for the Cappella Brancacci and its fresco cycle, and the Palazzo Pitti, home to a superb collection of Medici art and objects.

'I have seldom seen a city,' *wrote Percy Bysshe Shelley,* 'so lovely at first sight as Florence'

31

What to See in Florence

🏥 29D4
✉ Piazza San Giovanni,
   Piazza del Duomo
📞 055/230 2885 or 294 514
🕐 Mon–Sat 12–7, Sun and
   religious hols 8.30–2
   Closed 1 Jan, Easter Sun,
   24 Jun, 25–6 Dec
🍴 Nearby (€)
🚌 1, 6, 7, 11, 14, 23
♿ Good
💷 Inexpensive
↔ Campanile (▶ 33),
   Duomo (▶ 36–7), Museo
   dell'Opera del Duomo
   (▶ 44)

BATTISTERO ✪✪✪

The Baptistery of Florence was long believed to have been a Roman temple to Mars; the disovery of pavement fragments has confirmed the existence of a 1st-century palace on the site, though the core of the present building probably dates from the 6th–7th centuries. The marble decoration of the classically inspired exterior, remodelled in the 11th century, was to inspire generations of architects and provide the model for countless Tuscan churches.

The south doors (1328–36), the work of Andrea Pisano, depict scenes from the life of St. John the Baptist (the patron saint of Florence), and were cast by Venetian bell makers, then Europe's most accomplished bronze smiths. A famous competition was arranged in 1401 to award the commission for the north doors (1403–24), an event widely considered to have marked the 'beginning' of the Renaissance. It was won by Lorenzo Ghiberti, also responsible for the east doors (1425–52), works so exquisite they are often known as the 'Gates of Paradise' (the original panels are now in the Museo dell'Opera, ▶ 44).

Inside, the highlights are the mosaic ceiling (begun in 1225), created by Venetian mosaicists, and the glorious tessellated marble pavement, at whose heart you can still see the outlines of the building's original font (all Florentine children were once baptized here). Less eye-catching are the fine mosaic frieze; the lovely upper gallery and—to the right of the apse, or *scarsella*—the distinctive *Tomb of the Antipope John XXIII* (1427) by Donatello and Michelozzo.

The Baptistery's 13th-century mosaic ceiling is largely the work of Venetian craftsmen

CAMPANILE ★★

The multihued Campanile is one of Italy's most beautiful bell towers, and the views from its pinnacle are a highlight of any visit to Florence. At 85m (279ft), it is just 6m (20ft) lower than the Duomo, close by, and to reach the summit you have to climb 414 steps (there is no elevator).

Begun in 1334, the tower was probably designed by Giotto, who laboured on the project during his reign as city architect and *capo maestro* (head of works). At his death in 1337, however, only the base—the first of the tower's present five levels—was complete. Work on the second floor (1337–42) was supervised by Andrea Pisano, fresh from his work on the Baptistery's north doors. When he moved on, responsibility passed to Francesco Talenti, who completed the decoration and the remaining three floors (1348–59).

Most of the Campanile's many reliefs—probably designed by Giotto—are copies; the originals now reside in the Museo dell'Opera. Two sets decorate the first floor, the lower tier in hexagonal frames, the upper tier in diamonds. The hexagonal reliefs, by Pisano and his pupils, depict the Creation, the Arts and Industries and the Seven Sacraments. The Five Liberal Arts (Grammar, Philosophy, Music, Arithmetic and Astronomy) on the northern face are by Luca della Robbia. The upper reliefs, also the work of Pisano, portray the Seven Planets and Seven Virtues. On the second floor, the niche sculptures of the Sibyls and Prophets are copies of works by Donatello and others, now in the Museo dell'Opera.

🔲 29D4
✉ Piazza del Duomo
☎ 055/230 2885, 294 514 or 271 071
🕐 Apr–end Sep daily 8.30–5.40; Oct–end Mar Mon–Sat 8.30–6.40. Closing times indicate last admission: tower remains open 50 min thereafter. Closed 1 Jan, Easter Sun, 8 Sep, 25–6 Dec
🍴 Nearby (€)
🚌 1, 6, 7, 11, 14, 23
♿ None
💷 Expensive
↔ Battistero (▶ 32), Duomo (▶ 36–7), Museo dell'Opera del Duomo (▶ 44)

Climb to the top of Florence's famous bell tower for some superb views of the city

➕ 28A2
✉ Santa Maria del Carmine,
Piazza del Carmine
☎ 055/238 2195
🕐 Mon, Wed–Sat 10–5, Sun
and public hols 1–5.
Closed Tue, Easter Sun,
25 Dec
🍴 Nearby (€)
🚌 Shuttle bus B
♿ Few
💰 Moderate
↔ Giardino di Boboli (➤ 38),
Palazzo Pitti (➤ 48–9),
Ponte Vecchio (➤ 52)
❓ Entered via the cloisters
of Santa Maria del
Carmine (to the right of
the church façade)

CAPPELLA BRANCACCI

On its own, the church of Santa Maria del Carmine would merit little attention. Constructed between 1268 and 1422, it was almost completely rebuilt after a disastrous fire in 1771. One of the areas that survived the conflagration, however, was the Cappella Brancacci, a tiny chapel decorated with one of the most important and influential fresco cycles in Western art. It was commissioned in 1424 by Felice Brancacci, a former Florentine ambassador to Egypt, and its decoration entrusted to Masolino da Panicale (1383–1447) and his young assistant, Tommaso di Ser Giovanni di Mone Cassai (better known by his nickname Masaccio, or 'Mad Tom'). In 1426 Masaccio's burgeoning talents were given fuller rein when Masolino was recalled to Budapest, where he was employed as a painter to the Hungarian court.

In his absence Masaccio demonstrated a mastery of perspective, narrative drama and bold naturalism not seen in Florence since the days of Giotto. Masolino returned in 1427 but was called away to Rome a year later. Masaccio followed him after a few months, and neither painter worked in the chapel again. Masaccio died in the Holy City in 1428, aged just 28. In 1436 Brancacci was exiled by Cosimo de' Medici, leaving the frescoes untouched until their completion by Filippino Lippi in 1485. All but two of the frescoes depict scenes from the Life of St. Peter, and all of them are outstanding, but note in particular Masaccio's very powerful panel of *Adam and Eve Banished from Paradise* (top tier, extreme left). It is an excellent illustration of Masaccio's clever employment of stark and angular figures to portray profound emotion.

The Cappella Brancacci and its pioneering Renaissance fresco cycle

CASA BUONARROTI ⭐

The Casa Buonarroti, bought by Michelangelo in 1508, is often described as the sculptor's house (Michelangelo's surname was Buonarroti). In fact the maestro never lived here; the present house, its decoration and its collection of Michelangelo memorabilia were arranged by his nephew Leonardo (his sole descendant), and subsequently by Leonardo's son, Michelangelo the Younger. The house, if a little impersonal, is beautifully presented, its smart appearance the result of expensive restoration following the 1966 flood. The admission charge is a touch over-priced, however, especially given the fact that the museum contains only four minor works and a handful of drawings by the master. At the same time, the maze of decorated rooms, antique furniture, frescoed ceilings and various *objets d'art* are all attractive in their own right.

www.casabuonarroti
✚ 29F3
✉ Via Ghibellina 70
☎ 055/241 752
🕐 Mon, Wed–Sun 9.30–2.
 Closed Tue, 1 Jan,
 Easter Sun, 25 April, 1
 May, 15 Aug, 25–6 Dec
🍴 Nearby (€)
🚌 13, 19, 23, shuttle bus B
♿ Good
💶 Expensive
↔ Santa Croce (▶ 24)

The Battle of the Centaurs, *a marble relief by Michelangelo in the Casa Buonarroti*

The sculptural highlights are on the first floor. The earliest, the *Madonna della Scala* (1491), is a delicate, shallow relief showing the influence of Donatello. Carved when Michelangelo was still in his teens, it is 'the masters' earliest known work. Nearby stands the *Battle of the Centaurs* (1492), a more complex work executed when Michelangelo was employed by Lorenzo the Magnificent. The adjoining room features a wooden model of Michelangelo's plan for the façade of San Lorenzo (never realized), together with a sprawling wood-and-wax model of a torso, part of a huge river god possibly intended for the Cappelle Medicee. A room to the right contains a slender crucifix, a work believed lost until its discovery in 1965.

🕂 29D4
✉ Piazza del Duomo
☎ 055/230 2885, 271 071
or 294 514

DUOMO (SANTA MARIA DEL FIORE)   ✪✪✪

The first church on the site of Santa Maria del Fiore, Florence's magnificent cathedral, was built in the 7th century and dedicated to Santa Reparata, an obscure Syrian or Palestinian saint and martyr (San Lorenzo and the Baptistery served as Florence's cathedral for much of the city's early history). In the 13th century, when Florence was a prosperous and sophisticated metropolis, the city's elders declared the old church too 'crudely built and too

small for such a city'. They envisaged something to rival the new cathedrals of Siena and Pisa—something, as an edict of 1294 put it, of the 'most exalted and most prodigal magnificence, in order that the industry and power of men may never create or undertake anything whatsoever more vast and more beautiful'.

Responsibility for designing this magnificence was entrusted to Arnolfo di Cambio in 1294. After his death six years later, work lapsed until 1331; Giotto took over as the building's master of works in 1334. Construction of the vast Gothic nave, the tribunes (apses) and the drum of the colossal dome was finally completed in 1418.

The cathedral's interior is strikingly austere. It is also breathtaking in size—it can accommodate some 10,000 people—and ranks as Europe's fourth largest church after St. Peter's and the cathedrals of Milan and St. Paul's in London. The highlights include two large frescoed equestrian portraits on the north (left) wall: one of the English mercenary Sir John Hawkwood (1436) by Paolo Uccello, the other of Niccolò da Tolentino (1456)—another soldier of fortune—by Andrea del Castagno. Note, too, the clock above the main door by Paolo Uccello and the *Tomb of Antonio d'Orso* (1323) to its right, the work of Mino da Fiesole. Much of the stained glass in the apses was designed by Lorenzo Ghiberti, as was the superb reliquary (1432–42) in the middle (third) chapel of the central apse.

The cathedral's main highlight, however, is its vast dome, one of the supreme feats of late medieval engineering. Designed by Brunelleschi, who won the commission in 1418, it was built using many innovative techniques which are still shrouded in mystery. The key to the project's success was the construction of an inner and an outer shell, as well as the use of a herringbone pattern of bricks arranged in cantilevered rings (allowing the dome to support itself as it rose). Its interior is decorated with frescoes of the *Last Judgement* (1572–9) by Vasari, much criticized over the centuries as unworthy of so great a building. They pale into insignificance alongside the view from the dome's lantern, which is reached by steps from the top of the north (left) aisle.

GALLERIA DELL' ACCADEMIA (▶ 19, TOP TEN)

🕐 Cathedral and crypt Mon–Fri 10–5 (Thu 10–3.30), Sun 1.30–4.45,. 1st Sat of the month 10–3.30, otherwise Sat 10–4.45. Dome: daily 8.30–7.30 (shorter hours in winter)

🍴 Nearby (€)

🚌 1, 6, 7, 11, 14, 23

♿ Good

💶 Cathedral: free. Dome: expensive. Crypt: inexpensive

🔄 Campanile (▶ 33), Battistero (▶ 32), Museo dell'Opera del Duomo (▶ 44)

Did you know ?

The Duomo's façade and its striking Tuscan marbles—green from Prato, white from Carrara and red from the Maremma—is surprisingly recent. Arnolfo di Cambio's original façade, which was only a quarter finished, was pulled down in 1587, and replaced at the end of the 19th century following a competition in which some 92 designs were submitted.

Florence's beautiful marble-clad cathedral and its famous dome, one of the miracles of medieval engineering

GIARDINO DI BOBOLI

Italy's most popular gardens were begun in 1549, when the
Medici moved to the nearby Palazzo Pitti. They were
opened to the public in 1766. Today they are one of the
loveliest places in the city to rest, picnic or take a siesta.
They also offer sweeping views of the Florentine skyline,
notably from the belvederes beside the rococo *Kaffeehaus*
and the unkempt Giardino del Cavaliere. From the Palazzo
Pitti's main courtyard, where the gardens are entered,
paths lead to the Amphitheatre, a large arena designed to
house Medici entertainments (it was built over the quarry
used for the Palazzo's building stone). Sightseeing
highlights include many antique, Renaissance and
Mannerist statues; countless fountains (especially
Ganymede and *Neptune*); and the Viottolone, a long,
statue-lined avenue of cypresses which culminates in the
Isolotto, a pretty, moated island garden. The gardens also
contain the small Museo delle Porcellane, a collection of
antique porcelain, which can be visited on a combined
ticket with the gardens and Museo degli Argenti (►48–49).
Free maps of the garden (in Italian text) are sometimes
available on request at the ticket office.

*The Fontana del Nettuno
is one of many striking
fountains in the Boboli
Gardens; opposite, the
medieval kitchen of the
Antica Casa Fiorentina*

MUSEO DELLA ANTICA CASA FIORENTINA ✪✪

This beautiful medieval house offers a wonderful insight into how Florence's artists, merchants and noble families might once have lived as well as provides a vivid context for paintings and sculptures which can sometimes seem rather lifelessly displayed in the city's museums and galleries. The house was built in about 1330 for the Davizzi, a family of wealthy wool merchants. It was then sold to the Davanzati, who remained the owners until 1838. It opened as a museum in 1910 and was bought by the state in 1951.

In the entrance courtyard, which immediately sets the medieval tone, storerooms to the rear were kept stocked in case of siege or famine, while a private well served the house with water, a luxury in an age when most water was still drawn from public fountains. The age-old wooden staircase, the only one of its kind in Florence, leads to the first of the three floors, each of which is dotted with beautifully furnished rooms and evocative medieval corners.

Highlights of the first floor include the Sala dei Pappagalli, named after the parrots (*pappagalli*) adorning its frescoes, and the gorgeous Sala Pavoni or Camera Nuziale (Wedding Room). The latter features a glorious 14th-century Sicilian bedspread, a two-winged tabernacle by Neri di Bicci and a lovely frescoed frieze of trees, peacocks (*pavoni*) and exotic birds. The third floor is given over to the delightful palace kitchen, a room often situated on the upper floor of medieval houses to minimise damage in the event of fire.

✚ 28C3
✉ Palazzo Davanzati, Via Porta Rossa 13
☎ 055/238 8610
🕐 Call for times
🍽 Nearby in Piazza della Repubblica (€)
🚍 In the pedestrian zone: nearest services 6, 11, 31, 32, 37 to Piazza Santa Trínita
♿ Good
👆 Moderate
↔ Orsanmichele (▶46), Palazzo Vecchio (▶50), Piazza della Signoria (▶51), Ponte Vecchio (▶52), Santa Trínita (▶63),
❓ Museum closed for long-term restoration: consult tourist office for latest details

29E1
Piazza de' Mozzi 1
055/234 2427
Temporarily closed
Nearby on Lungarno
Serristori (€)
Shuttle buses B and C
Good
Moderate
Giardino di Boboli (➤
38), Palazzo Pitti
(➤ 48–49)

MUSEO BARDINI ⭐⭐

Unjustifiably ignored by most visitors, the Museo Bardini was created by Stefano Bardini, a 19th-century art dealer whose own collection became too large for his home, and was transferred to this ersatz 'palace' created from doors, ceilings and fireplaces salvaged from demolished medieval buildings.

The exhibits are housed in some 20 rooms ranged over two floors. On the ground floor rooms 7 and 8 feature some of the museum's highlights, notably a Cosmati pulpit, a tiny carved head attributed to Nicola Pisano, and a stunning Gothic *aedicule* (canopy) framing a statue of Charity by Tino da Camaino.

The first floor begins with armour and medieval weaponry before proceeding to Room 14, which features two of the collection's treasures: a terracotta *Madonna and Child* and the collage-like *Madonna dei Cordai*, both attributed to Donatello. Successive rooms offer a bewitching miscellany of reliefs, furniture and majolica. Room 20 boasts two magnificently inland choir stalls and one of the city's grandest wooden ceilings.

29E4
Via dell'Oriuolo 24
055/261 6545
Mon–Wed, Fri–Sun 9–2.
Closed Thu, 1 Jan, Easter
Sun, 1 May, 15 Aug,
25–6 Dec
Nearby (€)
14, 23, shuttle bus B
Few: garden approach
and some steps
Inexpensive
Museo Nazionale del
Bargello (➤ 22), Duomo
(➤ 36–37), Museo
dell'Opera del Duomo
(➤ 44)

MUSEO DI FIRENZE COM' ERA ⭐

This is one of the city's most interesting minor museums, thanks to a collection of paintings, engraving and topographical drawings evoking the Florence of days gone by. The first room contains its principal treasure, the *Pianta della Catena*, a vast panorama of the city as it appeared in 1470. The room to its right features lunette paintings (1599) of the Medici villas by the Flemish painter van Utens—among the loveliest things in any Florentine museum.

Other highlights include the engravings of Telemaco Signorini (1874) and a vaulted room devoted to drawings and engravings of the city's major buildings.

A lunette of a Medici villa in The Museo di Firenze com'era

A Walk from the Ponte Vecchio to San Miniato al Monte

This mainly uphill walk takes in some of the key sights of the Oltrarno and can easily be extended to embrace another three: the Palazzo Pitti (▶ 48–49), Giardino di Boboli (▶ 38) and Cappella Brancacci (▶ 34). As a less strenuous option, it can also be walked in reverse, downhill, by catching a 12 or 13 bus to Piazzale Michelangelo or San Miniato al Monte.

Cross the Ponte Vecchio and follow Via de' Guicciardini to Piazza Santa Felicita.

Santa Felicita, probably Florence's second oldest church after San Lorenzo, is noted for Brunelleschi's *Cappella Capponi*, celebrated in turn for Pontormo's *Deposition* (1525–8), a masterpiece of Mannerist painting.

Take the lane left of the church and turn immediately left to Via de' Bardi. Turn right and follow Via de' Bardi. Continue to Piazza de' Mozzi if you wish to visit the Museo Bardini. Otherwise turn right and dogleg up Costa Scarpuccia. Turn left on Costa di San Giorgio.

Number 19 Costa di San Giorgio was the home of Galileo. At the top of the street lies Porta San Giorgio (1258), the city's oldest surviving gateway. To the right is the entrance to the Forte di Belvedere (1590–95), built by Buontalenti for Ferdinand I. The views of the city from its ramparts are wonderful.

At Porta San Giorgio turn right and follow Via di Belvedere and the city walls for marvellous views over olive groves and the distant hills. At Porta San Miniato and the crossroads at the bottom turn right. After 150m (164yds) turn left on the stepped lane of Via di San Salvatore del Monte. This climbs past Stations of the Cross to Viale Galileo Galilei.

Turn left for Piazzale Michelangelo, a fine but often busy viewpoint. Turn right; after some 50m (164ft) steps and terraces lead off left to San Miniato al Monte. The 11th-century marble-clad church is worth a visit, and the views from here are also good if Piazzale Michelangelo below is rather crowded.

Distance
2km (1 mile)

Time
45 min or 2–3 hours with visits to churches, Museo Bardini and Forte del Belvedere

Start point
Ponte Vecchio
✚ 28C2

End point
San Miniato al Monte
✚ 29E1

Lunch
Cafés and restaurants with views on Viale Galileo Galilei, between Piazzale Michelangelo and San Miniato al Monte

Santa Felicita
✉ Piazza Santa Felicita
☎ 055/213 018
🕐 Daily 9–12, 3–6
♿ None
🎫 Free

Forte di Belvedere
✉ Costa di San Giorgio–Via di Belvedere
☎ 055/234 2822
🕐 Daily 9–dusk
♿ None
🎫 Free except during temporary exhibitions

Food & Drink

Poverty and peasant traditions have long inspired Tuscan cooking, with the result that the region's cuisine relies on simple, fresh ingredients and straightforward preparation and presentation. Simplicity is the keynote of most *antipasti* (starters), which include hams, salamis and *crostini* (small rounds of toasted bread with mushroom, olive, chicken liver and other pâté-like toppings).

Local specialties make ideal presents

Typical first courses (*primi*) are *pappardelle alla lepre* (noodles in a hare sauce); *pici*, a Sienese pasta; vegetable-based *minestrone*; *pappa al pomodoro*, a tomato and basil soup thickened with bread; *risotto*, often with the region's prized *porcini* mushrooms; and *ribollita*, a soup of beans, cabbage, vegetables and bread. Beans are so ubiquitous in the region's cuisine—notably in *zuppa di fagioli*—that other Italians lampoon the Tuscans as *mangiafagioli* (bean-eaters).

Main Courses

Meat and fish (on the coast) provide the focal point of most main courses (*secondi*). The best-known dish is the majestic *bistecca alla fiorentina*, a large T-bone steak drizzled with olive oil, seasoned with herbs and grilled over the embers of a chestnut-wood fire. Other grilled meats (*alla griglia*) are also common, especially lamb (*agnello*), pork (*maiale*) and chicken (*pollo*). Game and wild boar (*cinghiale*) are often available. A mixed grill is known as *arrosto misto*; a casserole-type sauce of meat, tomatoes and olives is known as *alla cacciatore* ('hunter-style'). Tuscan *scottiglia* is a stew of poultry, white wine and veal (*vitello*).

Puddings

Puddings can disappoint in restaurants, often because they are made off the premises or laced with a virulent liqueur. Most Tuscans plump for fresh fruit (*frutta fresca*)—grapes, strawberries, cherries—or stroll to a *gelateria* for an ice cream. Specialities include: *cantuccini*, almond biscuits dipped in dessert wine, or Siena's famous *panforte*, a combination of nuts and candied fruit. Cheese (*formaggio*) is also a good bet, especially sheep's cheese (*pecorino*).

Wine

Once upon a time Tuscan wine began and ended with Chianti. These days the region's wines are undergoing a renaissance, with many producers beginning to concentrate on high quality (and high-priced) wines. The grading system (DOC) is slightly discredited; many producers make wine independently, outside classification, known as *Vino da Tavola* and often better than DOC wine. Many are also experimenting with new grape varieties, blending French imports such as Cabernet Sauvignon with local staples such as Sangiovese (the grape used to make Chianti). *Sassicaia*, *Tignanello* and *Carmignano* are the best known of these 'Super Tuscans'.

Chianti is still the region's most famous wine, though two other great names offer more rewarding tipples if you can afford them: Brunello, from the area around Montalcino, is one of Italy's most majestic wines, produced by a bewildering array of tiny vineyards clustered around the ancient hill town. Its younger cousin, Rosso di Montalcino, is a less expensive but still outstanding alternative. Names to look out for include *Carpazo*, *Castello Romitorio* and the reasonably priced *Il Poggione*. Tuscany's other great wine is *Vino Nobile*, the ancient 'king of wines', produced around Montepulciano by estates such as Cantucci, Poliziano and Vecchia Cantina.

Reds have traditionally overshadowed the region's whites, the exceptions being *Galestro*, a light generic wine made by several producers, and *Vernaccia di San Gimignano*, which for years suffered a catastrophic fall in quality and prestige and is now making a comeback. Most *Vernaccia* sold in San Gimignano's shops, however, is insipid plonk. If you want quality go for wines from Guicciardini's Cusona estate, makers of *Vernaccia* for 500 years, Teruzzi & Puthod's *Carmen* and *Terra di Tufo*, and Falchini's *Casale* and *Vigna a Solatio*.

In October rural Tuscany is alive with the sights and sounds of the grape harvest

✚ 29D4

✉ Piazza del Duomo 9

☎ 055/230 2885

🕐 Apr–Oct Mon–Sat
9–7.30, Sun 9–1.40;
Nov–Mar Mon–Sat
9–5.20, Sun 9–1.40.
Closed 1 Jan, Easter Sun,
1 May, 15 Aug, 1 Nov, 8
Dec, 25–6 Dec

🍴 Nearby (€)

🚌 1, 6, 7, 11, 14, 23

♿ Good to ground floor only

✋ Expensive

↔ Bargello (➤ 22),
Battistero (➤ 32),
Campanile (➤ 33),
Duomo (➤ 36–37)

MUSEO DELL'OPERA DEL DUOMO

The Opera del Duomo was established in 1296 to supervise construction and maintenance of the cathedral and its many works of art. Today its sculpture collection ranks second only to the Bargello, having long housed artefacts removed for safekeeping from the Duomo, Baptistery and Campanile. The ground and mezzanine floors feature rooms filled with tools and models used during the Duomo's construction, together with sculpture removed from Arnolfo di Cambio's unfinished cathedral façade (demolished in 1587). Highlights from the latter include Donatello's *St. John*, the thickset *Madonna of the Glass Eyes* and the stiff-backed figure of *Pope Boniface VIII*. Donatello insisted on having a lock put on his workshop here after a rival sculptor had sneaked in to see his work in progress. Other parts of the museum feature models (1588) for the cathedral façade (none were ever realized); several illustrated volumes of choral music; and an octagonal chapel containing reliquaries and a lovely 14th-century altarpiece (1334).

The stairs to the upper floors feature Michelangelo's outstanding *Pietà* (1550), a fitting prelude to two superlative *cantorie*, or carved choir lofts, which dominate the floor's opening room. The loft on the left (1431–8), carved in white marble, is by Luca della Robbia, that on the right (1433–9), with a far more dramatic arrangement by Donatello. The room to the left features many age-

A piece of Roman sculpture in the courtyard of the Museo dell'Opera

blackened reliefs, also from the Campanile. In a room on the other side of the *cantorie* stands Donatello's extraordinary *Mary Magdalene*, while ranged around the walls are 16 statues removed from the Campanile. The museum's highlights, however, are the bronze panels crafted by Ghiberti for the Battistero doors, the focal point of paintings, mosaics and a glorious altarpiece (1459) by Antonio Pollaiuolo.

MUSEO DI SAN MARCO (➤ 23, TOP TEN)

MUSEO DI STORIA DELLA SCIENZA

Despite its fall from artistic grace after the Renaissance, Florence remained at the forefront of European science and learning, thanks to the work of men such as Galileo—born in nearby Pisa—and the enlightened patronage of rulers such as Ferdinand II and Cosimo II. This well-presented and unexpectedly fascinating museum captures the essence of the times, each of the many rooms (over two floors) being devoted to a separate scientific theme or discipline.

29D2
Piazza dei Giudici 1
055/265 311
Oct–end May Mon, Wed–Sat 9.30–5, Tue 9.30–1, 2nd Sun of month 10–1; Jun–end Sep Mon, Wed–Fri 9.30–5, Tue and Sat 9.30–1
Nearby (€)

The first floor opens with rooms devoted to counting machines and small instruments, including a case containing compasses which belonged to Michelangelo. Room 2's highlight is a beautifully enamelled quadrant; Room 3's is a lovely Tuscan astrolabe, two among hundreds of artefacts which display the Florentines' ability to turn even utilitarian objects into works of art. Room 4 features exhibits connected with Galileo, including the lens he used to discover the moons of Jupiter and—more bizarrely—some of the scientist's bones. Room 7, with its beautiful maps and globes, is one of the museum's loveliest corners.

The old microscopes of Room 9 lead to a salon devoted to the world's first scientific academy, the Accademia del Cimento, the body that—along with the Medici—was responsible for accumulating most of the museum's collection. Upstairs the museum delves into the mysteries of time and magnetism, followed by a sequence of less interesting pneumatic and hydrostatic displays. The best is saved until last: a roomful of alarming surgical instruments and horrifying anatomical waxworks.

23
Excellent
Expensive
Uffizi (▶ 26), Ponte Vecchio (▶ 52)
Loan of excellent free guides to each floor available on request (in four languages, including English)

Behind its austere façade the Museo di Storia della Scienza is one of Florence's most fascinating museums

✝ 29D3

✉ Orsanmichele: Via dei
Calzaiuoli (main entrance
to rear on Via dell'Arte
della Lana). Museum: Via
dell'Arte della Lana
(opposite church
entrance)

☎ 055/284 715

🕐 Temporarily closed at
time of writing check for
current times

🍴 Nearby (€)

🚌 In the pedestrian zone:
nearest services 1, 6, 7,
11, 14, 23

♿ Church: good. Museum:
none

✋ Free

↔ Battistero (➤ 32),
Campanile (➤ 33),
Duomo (➤ 36–37)

ORSANMICHELE ⭐⭐

Orsanmichele is one of Florence's most intimate churches,
providing a calm retreat from the crowds of Via dei
Calzaiuoli. The site's earliest church dates from 750, a
small chapel situated in the kitchen garden (*orto*) of a
Benedictine monastery. From these humble roots came its
present name, which is a contraction of *San Michele ad
Hortum* and *San Michele in Orto*. In 1280 the chapel was
replaced with a grain market, a building destroyed by fire in
1304. In 1380 this was replaced with another church, the
upper floor being retained as a granary.

Decoration of the new building was entrusted to the
city's leading guilds, each of which was asked to
commission a statue of its patron saint to adorn the
exterior. After years of delays, statues were eventually
secured from some of the greatest Renaissance artists,
among them Verrocchio, Ghiberti, Donatello and
Giambologna.

Some of these statues, such as Donatello's *St.
George*, have now been replaced with copies, the
originals removed for safekeeping to the church museum
and other city galleries. Others occupy their original niches
and have been cleaned as
part of a large on-going
restoration agenda. The
interior, however, retains
many of its oldest treasures,
not least a magnificent glass
and marble tabernacle
(1348–59) by Andrea
Orcagna, a work financed by
votive offerings that flooded
in after the Black Death of
1348. At its heart is a
Madonna and Child (1347), a
painting which is said to have
inherited the miracle-working
properties of a fresco on
the site, destroyed in the
fire of 1304. Most of the
interior's frescoes, which
were painted to complement
the exterior sculptures, show
the guild's patron saints.

The Madonna and Child *at the
heart of Andrea Orcagna's
sumptuous tabernacle*

PALAZZO MEDICI-RICCARDI ✪✪✪

To the average bystander this palace looks like just one more grime-covered Florentine *palazzo*. Built for Cosimo de' Medici in 1444, it was designed by Michelozzo, the Medici's leading architect, and remained the family's main home until Cosimo I moved to the Palazzo Vecchio in 1540. Its heavily rusticated ground-floor exterior, almost fortress-like in appearance, was to influence many Florentine buildings in the century of palace-building that followed. Today much of the mansion is occupied by council offices, making the survival of one of the city's most charming fresco cycles all the more remarkable.

Benozzo Gozzoli painted the three-panel *Journey of the Magi* (1459) for Piero de' Medici, probably in tribute to the Compagnia dei Magi, one of the city's leading religious confraternities (of which the Medici were leading members). Tucked away in the tiny Cappella dei Magi, the cycle has been restored to stunning effect. The three principal panels deal with one of the three kings of the Nativity, though most interest derives from Gozzoli's inclusion of contemporary portraits among the sea of faces. On the right wall, for example, the long procession is headed by a courtly figure probably intended to represent Lorenzo the Magnificent.

- 🗓 29D5
- ✉ Via Cavour 3
- ☎ 055/276 0340 or 276 0526
- 🕐 Thu–Tue 9–7
- 🍴 Nearby (€)
- 🚌 1, 6, 7
- ♿ None: several flights of stairs
- 🎟 Palace exterior and courtyard: free. Cappella dei Magi: moderate.
- ↔ Michelangelo's *David* (▶ 19), Battistero (▶ 32), Campanile (▶ 33), Duomo (▶ 36–7), Museo dell'Opera del Duomo (▶ 44), San Lorenzo (▶ 54–5)
- ❓ Tickets can be reserved in advance by phone or at the ticket office

Did you know ?

*Gozzoli included a self-portrait
in the right hand wall fresco.
He stands a couple of rows from the rear of the
procession with the words
OPUS BENOTI picked out in gold
on his red hat.*

*A sublime ornate ceiling
within the Palazzo Medici-
Riccardi*

47

✚ 28C1

✉ Piazza dei Pitti

☎ Galleria Palatina 055/238
8614. Museo degli
Argenti 055/238 8709 .
Galleria d'Arte Moderna
056/238 8601. Galleria
del Costume 055/238
8713

🕐 Galleria Palatina and
Apartaments Reali:
Tue–Sun 8.15–6.50;
Galleria del Costume and
d'Arte Moderna: Tue–Sat
and 1st, 3rd, 5th Sun and
2nd, 4th Mon of month
8.15–1.50; Museo degli
Argenti and Museo delle
Porcellane: daily
8.15–4.30/ 7.30. Closed
on public hols and 1st
and last Mon of month

🍴 Piazza dei Pitti (€)

🚌 36, 37, shuttle buses B
and C

♿ Good

🎟 Combined tickets for
Galleria Palatina and
Appartamenti
Monumentali, for Museo
degli Argenti, Museo
delle Porcellane and
Giardino di Boboli, and
for Galleria d'Arte
Moderna and Galleria del
Costume. Combined
tickets all moderate

🔁 Cappella Brancacci
(➤ 34), Giardino di Boboli
(➤ 38), Museo Bardini
(➤ 40), Ponte Vecchio
(➤ 52)

❓ Hours for the minor
museums change
constantly according to
the time of year, check
with the tourist office

PALAZZO PITTI ✪✪✪

Palaces and galleries do not come much larger than the Palazzo Pitti, home to the Medici for some 200 years and the setting for much of their private collection of paintings, silverware, costumes and miscellaneous objets d'art. The palace was begun in 1457 by Luca Pitti, a wealthy banker (possibly to a design by Brunelleschi), partly to upstage the Medici, then the Pitti's implacable rivals. By 1549 the Pitti had fallen on hard times, forcing them—ironically—to sell up to their old rivals. Once installed, the Medici altered the palace beyond recognition, adding two vast wings and countless additional rooms and salons.

These now house four separate museums, whose layout, ticketing and opening hours vary and can be slightly confusing. The main thing to see is the Galleria Palatina, home to a superlative collection of paintings (its entrance is to the rear right-hand side of the courtyard and up the stairs to the second floor). Within the Galleria, which is also something of a maze, you should start with the Sala di Venere, work down the following five state rooms, then return along the smaller parallel rooms to your starting point. The ceiling fresco in the Sala di Venere is the first of four, all by Piero da Cortona, each depicting allegorical and mythological scenes inspired by the Medici. The room also contains the first of the gallery's many exceptional paintings, which here (as elsewhere) are wedged from floor to ceiling with little attempt at classification. Critics often complain at the arrangement and poor labelling, though this provides a vivid illustration of the collection's size and is how the Medici Grand Dukes chose to display their paintings.

The Sala di Apollo contains one of the gallery's many masterpieces, Titian's *Portrait of a Gentleman* (1540), along with the same artist's sensuous *Mary Magdalene* (1531) and Van Dyck's portraits of *Charles I and Henrietta Maria*. The next room, the Sala di Marte, features Rubens' huge *Consequences of War* (1638), an allegory of the Thirty Years' War. The next room, the Sala di Giove, was once the grand-ducal throne room. Today it is home to one of Raphael's finest portraits, the *Donna Velata*, (*Veiled Woman*, 1516). More Raphaels line the walls of the next two rooms, including the famous *Madonna della Seggiola* (1515), along with works by Andrea del Sarto, Tintoretto, Giorgione, Perugino, Velázquez and others. Highlights of the parallel rooms include Crisofano Allori's celebrated *Judith and Holofernes*, Caravaggio's *Sleeping Cupid* and a sublime *Madonna and Child* by Filippo Lippi.

The most worthwhile of the Pitti's other museums is the Museo degli Argenti, whose lavish salons display the silverware, *pietra dura* vases and other priceless (if often tasteless) objects accumulated by the Medici. The Galleria d'Arte Moderna contains some 30 rooms of Tuscan paintings (1784–1945), the most interesting of which are by the *Macchiaioli* group, often called the Italian Impressionists. The Galleria del Costume has a sumptuous collection of clothes and costumes from the heyday of the Medici court.

The Palazzo Pitti contains countless sublime paintings and gloriously decorated rooms

The Palazzo Vecchio's
lovely courtyard was
designed by Michelozzo
and decorated by Vasari

✚ 29D2
✉ Piazza della Signoria
☎ 055/276 8465
🕐 Mon–Wed, Fri–Sun 9–7,
   Thu 9–2; last admission 1
   hour before closing.
   Closed Thu and 1 Jan,
   Easter Sun, 1 May, 15
   Aug, 25–6 Dec
🍽 Nearby (€)
🚌 In the pedestrian zone:
   nearest services 19, 23,
   31, 32
♿ Good
💶 Expensive (includes entry
   to Capella Brancacci)
↔ Uffizi (➤ 26),
   Orsanmichele (➤ 46),
   Piazza della Signoria
   (➤ 51)
❓ Hour-long tours
   (Mon–Sat; includes
   admission to palace) take
   visitors to parts of the
   palace normally closed:
   reserve in advance at
   ticket office

PALAZZO VECCHIO ★★

The Palazzo Vecchio (c1285–1322) served as Florence's
official seat of government for about seven centuries—it's
still the town hall. Designed by Arnolfo di Cambio, then also
employed on the Duomo, it was finished in 1303, but
radically altered by Cosimo I in 1540 when he moved the
Medici court here from the Palazzo Medici-Riccardi. When
Cosimo moved again in 1550, this time to the 'new' Palazzo
Pitti, the palace took its present name (vecchio means 'old').

Its courtyard (1453) was designed by Michelozzo, one
of the Medici's preferred architects, and later adorned by
Vasari with decorative panels to Medici prowess. Vasari
also built the staircase that leads to the palace's focal
point, the vast but soulless Salone dei Cinquecento, built in
1495 to accommodate the 500 members of Florence's
ruling assembly. Vasari decorated both its ceiling—whose
gilt-laden paintings glorify Cosimo I—and the walls, whose
six huge paintings (1563–5) depict a succession of
Florentine military triumphs. Beneath them may be a
series of unfinished frescoes begun in 1506 by
Michelangelo and Leonardo.

A statue of Victory (1525) by Michelangelo stands
almost opposite the Salone's entrance, while just off the
chamber is the tiny Studiolo (entrance door wall), a tiny but
exquisitely decorated room designed for Francesco I,
Cosimo's gloomy son. On the second floor enjoy the view
from the Terrazza di Saturno, the many decorated rooms—
notably Bronzino's Mannerist chapel—and the view of the
Piazza della Signoria from the Sala d'Udienza. The Sala dei
Gigli contains frescoes by Domenico Ghirlandaio and
Donatello's statue of Judith and Holofernes. Children will
enjoy the palace's innovative Museo dei Ragazzi.

PIAZZA DELLA SIGNORIA ✪✪

While the Piazza del Duomo was Florence's religious focus, the Piazza della Signoria has long served as the city's civic and political heart. Witness to countless momentous events across the centuries, such as the burning of Savonarola in 1498, it remains one of the city's busiest meeting places and the natural conclusion of the evening *passeggiata* (stroll) along Via dei Calzaiuoli. It was first enlarged in 1307 to accommodate the Palazzo dei Priori (now the Palazzo Vecchio), and was paved as early as 1385.

Sights include the Palazzo Vecchio; the Uffizi (off the square to the south); and the Loggia dei Lanzi, an outdoor gallery sheltering several outstanding pieces of sculpture. Greatest of these are Cellini's *Perseus* (1554) and Giambologna's contorted *Rape of the Sabine Women* (1583), though there are plans to replace these and other of the loggia's sculptures with copies.

More statues adorn the piazza itself: From left to right as you face the Palazzo Vecchio they include Giambologna's equestrian statue of *Cosimo I* (1587–94); the Neptune Fountain (1563–75) by Ammananti (the central figure of which was ridiculed by Michelangelo); next the *Marzocco*, a copy of Donatello's Florentine heraldic lion; *Judith and Holofernes* (1456–60), a copy of Donatello's statue in the Palazzo Vecchio; *David*, an 1873 copy of Michelangelo's most famous sculpture; and Bandinelli's *Hercules and Cacus* (1534), a work intended to symbolize Cosimo I, Florentine fortitude and the defeat of domestic enemies. On its unveiling the work was described by a fellow sculptor as a 'sack of melons'.

✚	29D3
✉	Piazza della Signoria
☎	None
🕐	Daily, 24 hours
🍽	Rivoire (▶ 57)
🚌	In the pedestrian zone: nearest services 19, 23, 31, 32
♿	Good
💵	Free
↔	Uffizi (▶ 26), Palazzo Vecchio (▶ 50)

Copies of famous sculptures stare down on Piazza della Signoria

+ 28C2
- ⊠ Ponte Vecchio
- ☎ None
- ⏰ Daily, 24 hours
- 🍴 Nearby (€–€€)
- 🚌 Pedestrianised
- ♿ Good
- 💲 Free
- ↔ Uffizi (➤ 26), Museo della Antica Casa Fiorentina (➤ 39), Palazzo Pitti (➤ 48), Palazzo Vecchio (➤ 50), Piazza della Signoria (➤ 51)
- ❓ Corridoio Vasariano occasionally open to visitors: consult Uffizi or tourist office for current opening times

The famous Ponte Vecchio has stood on the River Arno since 1345

PONTE VECCHIO ✪✪✪

The Ponte Vecchio and its huddle of old buildings are among the most familiar sights of Florence. Pitched close to the Arno's narrowest point, this is the last in a long succession of bridges on the site, dating back to Roman times. In 1944 it was the only Florentine bridge spared by the retreating Nazis, reputedly saved on Hitler's direct orders. In 1966 it was spared again—just—when it withstood the flood which brought death and destruction to much of Florence.

Until 1218 the bridge was the city's only river crossing, providing a vital lifeline between the old heart and the Oltrarno, on the Arno's southern bank. The present structure, which dates from 1345, was built to replace a bridge swept away in the floods of 1333 (some of the worst in the city's history). Its name ('Old Bridge') was coined to distinguish it from the Arno's other bridge, the Ponte alla Carraia, originally built in 1218.

Shops first appeared on the bridge during the 14th century, most of them butchers and fishmongers attracted by the river, a convenient dumping ground for offal and other refuse. The next arrivals were the tanners, who soaked hides in the river before adding to the communal stench by tanning them with horse's urine. Across the top of the shops runs the Corridoio Vasariano, built by Vasari to enable Cosimo I to walk undisturbed between his home (the Palazzo Vecchio) and offices (the Uffizi). In 1593 Ferdinand I raised shop rents and decreed that only jewellers and goldsmiths should occupy the bridge. They remain to this day.

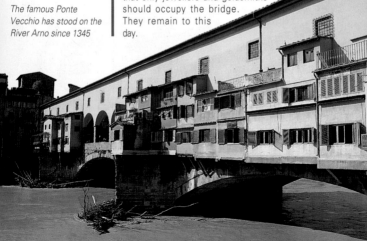

Santissima Annunziata's inner courtyard, the Chiostro dei Voti, is swathed in Renaissance frescoes

SANTISSIMA ANNUNZIATA ✪

The church of SS. Annunziata lies on one of Florence's lesser-known but most architecturally pleasing squares. Laid out by Brunelleschi in the 1420s, the area was altered several times over the next 200 years, the most notable additions being Giambologna's equestrian statue of Ferdinand I (1608) and two bizarre little fountains, the work of Giambologna's pupil, Pietro Tacca.

The church, which dominates the piazza's northern flanks, was built to praise the Annunciation, a crucial event in the life of the city: In the old Florentine calendar, the New Year began on the Feast of the Annunciation (25 March). It is now the mother church of the Servites, an order founded in 1234 by would-be servants (*servi*) of the Virgin.

The order built a chapel, which began drawing the crowds after 1252, when a painting begun by a Servite monk was miraculously completed by an angel. By 1450 so many pilgrims were coming that a new church, paid for by the Medici, was commissioned to house the painting. Via dei Servi was built at the same time to link SS. Annunziata and the Duomo, the two most important churches in the city dedicated to the Virgin.

The church's main sight is the inner courtyard, the Chiostro dei Voti (1447), swathed in frescoes by Andrea del Sarto, Jacopo Pontormo and Rosso Fiorentino. Inside the main body of the church lies Michelozzo's magnificent Tempietto (1448–61), built to shelter the miraculous painting. The first two chapels on the left feature celebrated works by Andrea del Castagno.

SANTA CROCE (▶ 24, TOP TEN)

✚ 29E5
✉ Piazza della Santissima Annunziata
☎ 055/266 181
🕐 Daily 7.30–12.30, 4–6.30
🍴 Nearby (€–€€)
🚌 6, 31, 32
♿ Good 🎟 Free
↔ *David*, Galleria dell'Accademia (▶ 19), Museo di San Marco (▶ 23), Palazzo Medici-Riccardi (▶ 47)
❓ The eastern side of Piazza della SS. Annunziata is dominated by a loggia (1493) built by Brunelleschi for the **Ospedale degli Innocenti**, Europe's first orphanage. The Ospedale's small Renaissance art collection and contrasting 'Men's' and 'Women's' cloisters are open to the public

Ospedale degli Innocenti
✉ Piazza della Santissima Annunziata 12
☎ 055/249 1708
🕐 Mon, Tue, Thu–Sun 8.30–2, 1st Sun of month 8.30–4. Closed 1 Jan, Easter Sun, 1 May, 15 Aug, 25–6 Dec
🎟 Inexpensive

SAN LORENZO ✪✪✪

San Lorenzo was founded in 393, making it one of the oldest churches in Florence. It served as the city's cathedral until the 7th century. A Romanesque church built on the site in 1060 survived until 1419, when Giovanni de' Medici and a group of parishioners offered to pay for a new church. Brunelleschi, then working on the Duomo, started work two years later, but progress faltered in the face of political and financial upheavals and only resumed when Giovanni's son, Cosimo de' Medici, offered 40,000 florins to ensure its completion (150 florins at this time could support a family for a year). As a result, the church became the Medici's dynastic church, while its rear portion, the Cappelle Medicee, became their private chapel (➤ 17).

The interior is an early Renaissance masterpiece. Brunelleschi created 'sails' of creamy wall interspersed with austere grey *pietra serena*. Artistic highlights include Rosso Fiorentino's *Marriage of the Virgin* (second altar on the right) and Desiderio da Settignano's *Pala del Sacramento* (1451–68), on the wall at the end of the right nave.

In the middle of the church stand two raised pulpits (1455–66), among the last works of Donatello (and pupils), and in front of the high altar brass grilles mark the tomb of Cosimo de' Medici (with a plaque inscribed *Pater Patriae*—

Father of the Fatherland). The *Martyrdom of St. Laurence* (1565–9), left of the two pulpits, is a graphic painting by Bronzino. In a chapel round the corner is a cenotaph to Donatello, who died in 1464 and was buried near Cosimo, his friend and patron. Brunelleschi's Sagrestia Vecchia, or Old Sacristy (1421), a simple architectural gem, is entered from the left transept of the church. On the left as you enter stands the bronze and porphyry tomb of Giovanni and Piero de' Medici (Cosimo de' Medici's sons), and in the middle is the tomb of Giovanni and Piccarda, Cosimo's parents and founders of the Medici fortune.

Most of the sacristy's decoration (1434–43) is by Donatello, most notably the eight tondi showing the Evangelists and scenes from the life of St. John (Giovanni's patron saint). The reliefs above the doors of the end wall portray Cosmos and Damian, the Medici's patron saints, and saints Laurence and Stephen, protectors of Florence.

From the church cloisters, stairs lead to the Biblioteca Laurenziana,

Did you know ?

St. Laurence (San Lorenzo), was a 3rd-century Roman martyr, roasted alive on a grid-iron because when the Romans had ordered him to collect 'all the treasures of the Church', Laurence had gathered all the sick and poor people he could find. During his roasting he apparently told his tormentors they could turn him over: 'I am done on this side'.

begun in 1524 to house the Medici's vast 100-year old library, collected by agents sent as far afield as Germany and the Middle East. Michelangelo designed the Ricetto (Vestibule), with its revolutionary use of space, and almost every detail of the library Reading Room—even the desks. The four rooms beyond contain a fraction of the books and manuscripts.

Above: *Statues by Michelangelo in the Cappelle Medicee*
Left: *The cloisters of San Lorenzo*

In the Know

If you only have a short time to visit Tuscany and Florence, or want to get a real flavour of the region, here are some ideas:

10

Ways to Be A Local

Join the evening *passeggiata* (stroll) in Via dei Calzaiuoli.

Drink espresso after lunch or dinner—the Italians *never* have cappuccino with a meal.

Visit *Vivoli* at Via Isola delle Stinche 7r for the best ice cream in Florence (see below).

Buy your stationery from *Pineider* in Piazza della Signoria.

Join the locals on Sunday to watch Fiorentina, Florence's soccer team.

Take an afternoon siesta on hot summer afternoons.

Don't make a *brutta figura*—an 'ugly image' or fool of yourself—by dressing badly or drinking too much.

Take a Sunday morning stroll in the Giardino di Boboli.

Make an extra effort with your appearance when you're dining out.

Do your shopping in the old Mercato Centrale.

10

Good Places to Have Lunch

Antellesi (€–€€) Via Faenza 9r ☎ 055/216 990: an easygoing place with simple wooden tables and traditional dishes.

Belle Donne (€–€€) ✉ Via delle Belle Donne 16r ☎ 055/238 2609: a tiny and genial restaurant with shared tables and eye-catching interior.

Cantinetta Antinori (€€) ✉ Piazza Antinori 3 ☎ 055/292 234: elegant and beautiful wine bar with a lively atmosphere.

Cantinetta dei Verrazzano (€€) ✉ Via dei Tavolini 18–20r ☎ 055/268 590: nice wine bar with marble-topped tables and tasty Tuscan snacks.

Casalinga (€) ✉ Via dei Michelozzi 9r ☎ 055/218 624: authentic Oltrarno trattoria, popular with locals and visitors alike.

Cibreo (€€) ✉ Via del Verrocchio 8 118r ☎ 055/234 1100: have lunch in the less expensive bistro to the rear of the main restaurant.

Da Ganino (€–€€) ✉ Piazza dei Cimatori 4r ☎ 055/214 125: central, reasonably priced restaurant with outside tables.

Il Cantinone del Gallo Nero (€) ✉ Via Santo Spirito 6r ☎ 055/218 898: wine bar in vaulted cellar with a choice of starters and hot and cold snacks.

Latini (€) ✉ Via dei Palchetti, off Via della Vigna Nuova ☎ 055/210 916: a busy trattoria with crowded tables and raucous atmosphere.

Le Volpi e L'Uva (€–€€) ✉ Piazza dei Rossi 1r ☎ 055/239 8132: a refined and delightful wine bar with a wide variety of wines and cold snacks.

10

Good Places for Snacks, Coffee or Cakes

Caffè Amerini (€) ✉ Via della Vigna Nuova 63r ☎ 055/284 941: intimate brick-arched interior. Good salads, sandwiches and snacks.

Daria (€) ✉ Borgo degli Albizi 36r ☎ 055/234 0979: a third generation family-run bar and Florentine institution dating from the 1940s.

Giacosa (€€) ✉ Via della Spada 10r ☎ 055/277 6328: sophisticated 19th-century bar where the Negroni cocktail was born; also renowned for its marrons glacés and other confectionery.

Gilli (€€) ✉ Via Roma 1r–Piazza della Repubblica 39r ☎ 055/239 6310: Florence's oldest and grandest bar; the most tempting of the four famous cafés on Piazza della Repubblica.

Giubbe Rosse (€€) ✉ Piazza della Repubblica 13–14r ☎ 055/212 280: celebrated 19th-century literary café; one of Piazza della Repubblica's historic bars.

Manaresi (€) ✉ Via de' Lamberti 16r ☎ None: thought by many to serve Florence's best cup of coffee.

Pasticceria Robiglio (€) ✉ Via dei Servi 112r ☎ 055/212 784 or 214 501 ✉ Via Tosinghi 11r ☎ 055/215 013: a family-run Florence institution founded in the 1920s: its two outlets sell some of the city's best cakes and confectionery.

Paszkowski (€€) ✉ Piazza della Repubblica 6r ☎ 055/210 236: venerable and much feted Piazza della Repubblica café.

Procacci (€–€€) ✉ Via dei Tornabuoni 64r ☎ 055/211 656: smart bar known for its legendary *panini tartufati* (truffle purée sandwiches).

Rivoire (€€) ✉ Piazza della Signoria 5r ☎ 055/214 412: expensive and well-known bar with outside tables on the main square.

5
Good Places for Ice Cream

Bondi (€) ✉ Via Nazionale 61r ☎ 055/287 490: offers some exotic and occasionally eccentric flavours and combinations of tastes.

Carabé (€) ✉ Via Ricasoli 60r ☎ 055/289 476: after seeing *David* in the nearby Accademia, come here for a *granita* (crushed ice with a choice of fruit syrup) or a tub of the excellent pistachio ice cream.

Festival del Gelato (€) ✉ Via del Corso 75r ☎ 055/294 386: choice is the main problem at this gelateria, which offers over 100 flavours.

Perchè No! (€) ✉ Via dei Tavolini 19r ☎ 055/239 8969: a central *gelateria* that has been in business since 1939.

Vivoli (€) ✉ Via Isole delle Stinche 7r ☎ 055/292 334: quite simply the best ice cream in Florence—perhaps even in Italy.

5
Best Tuscan Views

- From the Campanile, Florence.
- From the Torre del Mangia in the Palazzo Pubblico, Siena.
- From the walls of the hilltop village of Pienza.
- From the Torre dei Guinigi, Lucca.
- From the Torre Grossa, San Gimignano.

10
Top Activities

Bicycling: bicycles can be hired in Florence and most large towns. Contact individual tourist offices for details.

Canoeing: for information ontact the Federazione Italiana Canoa; (☎ 055/689 044; www.federcanoa.it).

Caving: excellent opportunities in the Alpi Apuane: contact the Gruppo Speleologico Fiorentino, (☎ 055/660 754; www.gsfi.da.ru).

Diving: off the coast and islands of the Tuscan Archipelago: contact the Federazione Italiana Attività Subacquee (FIAS), www.fipsas.it

Fishing: plenty of coastal and sea fishing; Contact local tourist offices for details of conditions, permits and tackle shops.

Horseback riding: riding and pony-trekking are widely available throughout Tuscany: most tourist offices carry lists of local venues.

Mountaineering: in the Alpi Apuane, Orecchiella and elsewhere. Most towns have a branch office of the Club Alpino Italiano (CAI): contact tourist offices for local addresses. The Florence office is at Via del Mezzetta 2/M (☎ 055/612 0467; www.caifirenze.it).

Skiing: winter sports are available, snow allowing, around Abetone, to the northeast of Lucca.

Windsurfing: off the coast and islands of the Tuscan archipelago, notably Elba. Contact the Associazione Surfisti Italiani Versilia, Via Nino Bixio 30, 55049 Viareggio (LU), Tuscany (☎ 0584 55 074).

Walking: for the best-organized accompanied and self-guided walking holidays in Tuscany contact ATG–Oxford, 69–71 Banbury Road, Oxford, UK (☎ 01865 315678; www.atg-oxford.co.uk).

■ 28B4
✉ Piazza Santa Maria Novella
☎ Church: 055/215 918. Museum: 055/282 187
🕐 Santa Maria Novella: Mon–Thu 9–5, Fri 1–5, Sat 9–5, Sun 1–5. Museo di Santa Maria Novella: Mon–Thu, Sat 9–5, Sun 9–2. Closed Fri and 1 Jan, Easter Sun, 25 Apr, 1 May, 15 Aug, 25–6 Dec
🍴 Nearby in Piazza Santa Maria Novella (€)
🚌 All services to the rail station
♿ Good
💷 Santa Maria Novella: free. Museo di Santa Maria Novella: inexpensive
↔ Cappelle Medicee (▶ 17), Santa Trínita (▶ 63)
❓ Guided tours of the church occasionally available

SANTA MARIA NOVELLA

Santa Maria Novella ranks second only to Santa Croce in the pantheon of great Florentine churches. Begun as a simple chapel in the 9th century, it was rebuilt in 1094 and christened Santa Maria delle Vigne (Mary of the Vineyards). It then passed to the Dominicans, who in 1246 began a new church. The Romanesque façade was not finished until 1456, when Leon Battista Alberti completed the multi-hued frontage.

The lofty Gothic interior has several important frescoes, the most famous of which is Masaccio's *Trinità* (1428), midway down the left wall, one of the first Renaissance paintings to put the new theories of perspective to good use. Close by is Brunelleschi's pulpit (1443–52), where the Inquisition first denounced Galileo for agreeing with Copernicus that the earth revolved around the sun, and not vice versa.

Many of the church's chapels were commissioned by leading Renaissance businessmen. Banker Filippo Strozzi employed Filippino Lippi to fresco the Cappella di Filippo Strozzi with scenes from the life of his namesake, St. Philip (Filippo) the Apostle. The chapel to its right, the Cappella Bardi, features faded 14th-century frescoes, some attributed to Cimabue, Giotto's first teacher.

To the left of the Strozzi chapel, in the chancel, is Domenico Ghirlandaio's beautiful fresco cycle on the *Life of the Virgin* (left wall) and *Life of St. John the Baptist* (right wall). Despite their religious themes, these are actually vignettes of daily life in 15th-century Florence; they were commissioned by another banker, Giovanni Tornabuoni, whose relations appear in several scenes.

More frescoes (1351–7), the work of Nardo di Cione, adorn the Cappella Strozzi (up steps at the top left-hand side of the church): *Paradiso* (left wall); the *Last Judgement* (behind the altar) and a map-like *Inferno* (right wall), a commentary on Dante's epic poem *The Divine Comedy*. The altarpiece is by Nardo's brother, Andrea di Cione, better known as Orcagna, and shows *Christ Giving the Keys to St. Peter and the Book of Knowledge to Thomas Aquinas* (the chapel is dedicated to Aquinas).

Left of Santa Maria's façade is the entrance to the church museum and Chiostro Verde (Green Cloister), named after the green pigment of its badly faded frescoes. Despite the deterioration, many of the panels are superb—especially Paolo Uccello's *Universal Deluge* (1430), whose lurching composition illustrates his obsession with perspective. Notice the arks to either side of the picture, depicted before and after the Flood.

Off the cloister lies the Cappellone degli Spagnuoli, once used by the Spanish entourage of Eleanor of Toledo, wife of Cosimo I. It features one of the city's most striking fresco cycles, the work of Andrea da Firenze.

The left wall shows *The Triumph of Doctrine*, with Thomas Aquinas enthroned amidst the Virtues and Doctors of the Church.

The right wall portrays *The Work and Triumph of the Dominican Order*, with St. Dominic unleashing the 'hounds of the Lord' (*Domini canes*, a pun on 'Dominicans'). The four women are the Four Vices, surrounded by dancing and other debaucheries. A nearby friar hears confessions before sending the saved heavenwards; above the kneeling pilgrims are portraits of Dante, Petrarch, Giotto and others.

Santa Maria Novella's façade was completed 200 years after the church was begun

A Walk around Fiesole

Distance
2.5km (1.5 miles) one way

Time
Allow a morning

Start point
Piazza Mino da Fiesole
 65D5

End point
Badia Fiorentina or Piazza Mino da Fiesole
65D5

Tourist office: Via Portigiani 3 (☎ 055/598 720; www. comune.fiesole.fi.it)

7 ATAF bus from Florence rail station, Piazza San Marco or Via Martelli (near the Duomo) to Piazza Mino da Fiesole. Services call at San Domenico di Fiesole, near the Badia Fiesolana, for the return to Florence.

Lunch
Cafés around Piazza Mino da Fiesole (€)

Teatro Romano–Museo Archeologico
✉ Via Portigiani 1
☎ 055/59 477
🕓 Apr–Sep daily 9:30–7; Mar and Oct 9.30–6. Closed Tue Nov–Feb
Moderate
Museum ticket includes entrance to the Antiquarium Costantini

Museo Bandini
✉ Via Dupré 1
☎ 055/59 477
🕓 Apr–Sep daily 10–7; Nov–Feb Mon, Wed–Sat 10–5, Sun 10–7
Moderate
Combined ticket includes access to all Fiesole's museums

The ancient hill town of Fiesole nestles in the hills above Florence, providing a tranquil retreat from the city during the dog days of summer. It is a popular destination on weekends, so be prepared for crowds.

Start in Piazza Mino da Fiesole and take Via Marini to the right of the Duomo to the Museo Bandini and archaeological zone.

The Cappella Salutati in the Duomo features two works by Mino da Fiesole: the *Tomb of Bishop Salutati* and an altar-frontal of the *Madonna and Child*. The cathedral's high altar has an impressive altarpiece by Bicci di Lorenzo. Off Via Marini lie the 1st-century BC Teatro Romano, the Museo Archeologico and the ruins of Etruscan walls and temples. The Antiquarium Costantini, in Via Portigiani, contains a fine collection of Greek vases. The Bandini museum houses early Florentine paintings. There is a combined museum ticket available that includes admission to the Antiquarium Costantini.

Return to Piazza Mino da Fiesole and take Via San Francesco off its northwest flank. Walk uphill to see San Francesco and Sant'Alessandro, returning to the piazza the way you came or via the parallel/nearby woodland path.

Sant'Alessandro, one of the town's loveliest buildings, was built in the 6th century over the site of Roman and Etruscan temples. San Francesco enjoys breezy views of Florence and has an important 15th-century painting, *The Immaculate Conception*, by Piero di Cosimo.

From the Piazza take Via Vecchia Fiesolana past the Villa Medici to San Domenico. Turn right on Via Badia dei Roccettini to the Badia Fiesolana.

San Domenico contains a *Madonna and Child with Angels* (1430) by Fra Angelico; the chapter house (number 4) has a *Crucifixion* by the same artist. The Badia features a lovely 11th-cenutury façade incorporated into a 15th-century frontage. Its interior is styled in the manner of Brunelleschi. This was Fiesole's original cathedral.

Tranquil Fiesole nestles in the hills above Florence, providing superb views across the city

✚ 29E1
✉ Off Viale Galileo Galilei
☎ 055/234 2731
🕐 Summer daily 8–7.30;
   winter Mon–Sat 8–12,
   3–6, Sun 3–6
🍴 Nearby in Viale Galileo
   Galilei (€–€€)
🚌 12, 13
♿ Good, but steps to parts
   of church
✋ Free

SAN MINIATO AL MONTE

The most beautiful church in Florence takes its name from St. Minias, an Oriental Christian merchant who was martyred in Florence in AD250. According to legend the saint picked up his severed head and carried it from his place of execution (close to Piazza della Signoria) across the Arno to the hilltop site where his church now stands. Most of the present building dates from 1013, making it among the city's oldest churches.

The Romanesque façade (1090–1270) features a mosaic of Christ, Mary and St. Minias (1260) and a gilded eagle clasping a bale of wool—symbol of the Arte di Calimala, the wealthy guild which was made responsible for the church's fabric in 1228.

The breathtaking interior is dominated by a sumptuous painted wooden ceiling (1322) and a famous inlaid pavement (1207), reputedly inspired by Sicilian fabrics, and patterned with lions, doves and the signs of the zodiac. The capitals on the pillars of the nave are Roman and Byzantine originals. In the left-hand aisle is the Cappella del Cardinale del Portogallo, a Renaissance masterpiece complete with paintings, glazed terracotta and funerary sculpture, the works of sculptor Antonio Rossellino and painters Baldovinetti and two brothers Antonio and Pietro Pollaiuolo. The Cardinal of Portugal, whose uncle was King of Portugal, died in Florence in 1459. At the end of the nave, alongside Michelozzo's free-standing Cappella del Crocifisso (1448), steps lead to the raised choir and a magnificent carved pulpit and screen (1207). The sacristy, off to the right boasts a vivid fresco cycle by Spinello Aretino depicting Scenes from the Life of St. Benedict (1387).

Part of San Miniato's breathtaking interior

Santa Trínita's distinctive baroque façade masks a more austere Gothic interior

SANTA TRÍNITA ⊕

Santa Trínita is something of an architectural curiosity. Its flamboyant baroque exterior makes a striking contrast with the calm, Gothic assurance of its interior. Founded in 1092, it was rebuilt between 1258 and 1280—possibly to a design by Nicola Pisano—and the façade was added by Buontalenti in 1593.

The dusky, atmospheric interior has several wonderful works of art, most notably Domenico Ghirlandaio's frescoes (1483) in the Cappella Sassetti (the right-hand chapel to the right of the high altar). They represent episodes from the life of St. Francis and were commissioned by Francesco Sassetti in a bid to outdo his rival, Francesco Tornabuoni, who had paid for the frescoes in Santa Maria Novella, also by Ghirlandaio.

The panel portraying *St. Francis Receiving the Rule* in the lunette above the altar is famous for its setting—the Piazza della Signoria—and its portraits, which include Sassetti, who worked for the Medici bank, between his son, Federigo, and Lorenzo the Magnificent. On the stairs stand the humanist Poliziano and three of his pupils, the sons of Lorenzo the Magnificent.

The chapel's altarpiece, also by Ghirlandaio (1485), depicts *The Adoration of the Magi*, combining classical and Christian motifs (notice the Roman sarcophagus). Sassetti and his wife are portrayed to either side. Other works of art include Lorenzo Monaco's early 15th-century frescoes (fourth chapel on the right), the *Tomb of Bishop Federighi* (1454–7) by Luca della Robbia (second chapel left of the altar) and frescoes by Neri di Bicci and Bicci di Lorenzo (fourth chapel on the left).

UFFIZI, GALLERIA DEGLI (▶ 26, TOP TEN)

➕ 28B3
✉ Piazza di Santa Trínita
☎ 055/216 912
🕐 Mon–Sat 8–12, 4–6, Sun 4–6. Summer hours may be longer
🍴 Nearby (€)
🚌 6, 11, 31, 32, 36, 37
♿ Good
🎟 Free
↔ Museo della Antica Casa Fiorentina (▶ 39), Ponte Vecchio (▶ 52), Santa Maria Novella (▶ 58–59)

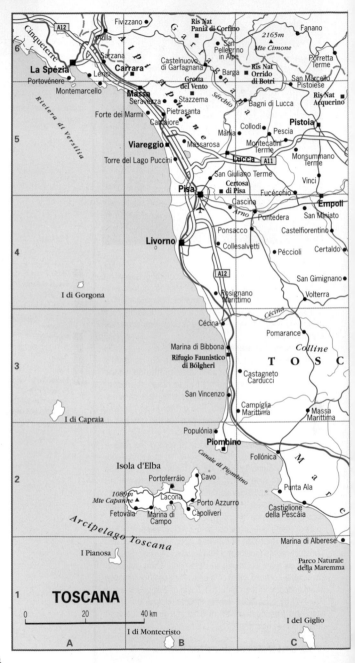

TOSCANA

0   20   40 km

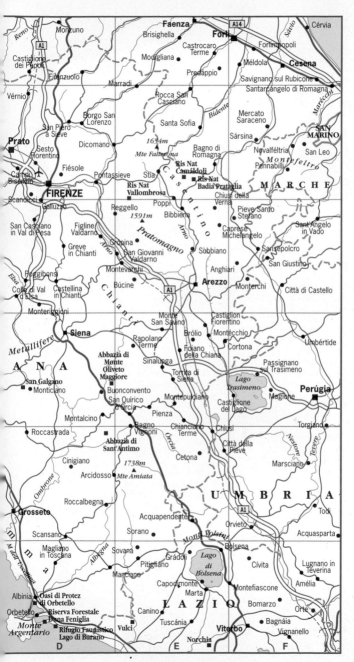

Tuscany

Tuscany is Italy at its best, a region of lovely medieval hill towns, sleepy villages and cypress-ringed villas and farmhouses. Vineyards, olives and fields of sunflowers mingle with rambling wooded hills, ragged mountains and sunbaked plains to form landscapes of timeless beauty. Art and culture are everywhere, from dusty Madonnas in half-forgotten churches to frescoes in majestic hilltop monasteries. And then there's the food and wine—as alluring as any number of paintings and hilltop towns.

Siena is the region's premier town, home to some of the most attractive medieval streets, museums and galleries in Italy; Lucca is a wonderfully gracious and civilized little town, and nearby Pisa has its famous tower and cathedral. Cortona and Montepulciano are charming towns, full of medieval corners and splendid views. Among the villages, San Gimignano stands out, thanks to its beautiful tower-filled medieval skyline.

'A place overflowing with everything that makes for ease, for plenty, for beauty, for interest and good example'

HENRY JAMES,
Italian Hours (1909)

———●———

Lucca, viewed from the Torre Guinigi

What to See in Tuscany

AREZZO ⊗

This largely modern town merits a visit if only for Piero della Francesca's *The Legend of the True Cross* (1452–66), one of Italy's most famous fresco cycles. Ranged across the chancel of **San Francesco**, a church at the heart of the old town, the cycle describes how the tree from which Eve plucked the forbidden fruit becomes the cross of Christ's crucifixion. Although damaged in places, the frescoes have been restored, emphasizing the calm tones and subtlety for which Piero is renowned.

Make sure you also visit the Piazza Grande, the town's precipitously sloping main square, which is graced by the Loggia di Vasari (1573) and Palazzetto della Fraternità della Laici, built for a lay confraternity and distinguished by a beautiful doorway and lunette tabernacle (1434) by Bernardino Rossellino. To its left protrudes the arcaded apse of Santa Maria, a lovely Romanesque church whose façade looks over the nearby Corso Italia. The interior has a superb altarpiece (1320) by Pietro Lorenzetti.

To the north stands the **Duomo**, whose airy Gothic interior is known for Piero della Francesca's fresco of *Mary Magdalene* and 14th-century *Tomb of Bishop Guido Tarlati* (end of the north aisle). Also worth a look are the cathedral museum, filled with paintings, sculpture and terracotta; the nearby **Casa Vasari**, birthplace of the 16th-century painter and writer; and the **Museo d'Arte Medievale e Moderna**, with an eclectic assortment of paintings and objects, including five rooms of ceramics and paintings by the *Macchiaioli*, the so-called 'Italian Impressionists'.

✚ 65E4

San Francesco
✉ Piazza San Francesco
☎ 0575/302 001 or
 0575/352 727;
 www.ticketeria.it
🕓 Mon–Fri 9–6, Sat 9–5.30,
 Sun 1–5.30. Prebooked
 guided tours every 30
 minutes
♿ Good
🎟 Moderate. Tickets must
 be prebooked by phone
 or (off-season) in person
 an hour before visit

Duomo
✉ Piazza del Duomo
☎ 0575/23 991
🕓 Daily 7/8.30–12.30,
 3–6.30/7
♿ Few
🎟 Free

Casa Vasari
✉ Via XX Settembre 55
☎ 0575/40901
🕓 Mon–Sat 9–7, Sun 9–1
♿ Few
🎟 Free

Museo d'Arte Medievale e Moderna
✉ Via di San Lorentino 8
☎ 0575/409050
🕓 Tue–Sun 9–7. Closed
 Mon and 1 Jan, 1 May,
 25 Dec
♿ Few
🎟 Moderate

ℹ Tourist office: Piazza della
 Repubblica 28
 (☎ 0575/377 678;
 www.apt.arezzo.it).

The Piazza Grande, with Santa Maria's arcaded apse and Rossellino's beautiful Renaissance doorway

CORTONA ⭐⭐

Etruscan Cortona is a beguiling little hill town, with ancient walls ringed with olives and vineyards and twisting cobbled lanes and belvederes giving sweeping views over the surrounding countryside. A short walk from Piazza della Repubblica, which forms the heart of the old town, leads to the **Museo Diocesano**, a museum noted for its handful of marvellous Renaissance paintings. The best-known are the glorious *Annunciation* (1428–30) and *Madonna Enthroned with Saints*, both by Fra Angelico, together with works by Pietro Lorenzetti, Sassetta, Bartolomeo della Gatta and the local-born Luca Signorelli.

The town's other major gallery is the excellent **Museo dell'Accademia Etrusca**, packed with a wide-ranging collection of Etruscan objects, Renaissance ivories, porcelain, ceramics, miniatures, coins and jewellery. Its highlights are an unusual 5th-century BC Etruscan 'chandelier' and a reconstructed Etruscan tomb, (on the upper floor).

You should also visit San Niccolò, a church approached through a charming little walled garden and dominated by an intriguing double-sided altarpiece by Luca Signorelli. San Domenico has another work by Signorelli, a *Madonna and Saints*, while San Francesco boasts a fine *Annunciation* by Pietro da Cortona, another local painter. Some way outside the walls stands Santa Maria del Calcinaio, a distinguished but rather austere Renaissance church. A far better destination if you want to stretch your legs is the Fortezza Medicea, a ruined Medici fortress at the top of the town, which offers sensational views across Lake Trasimeno and the Umbrian hills.

🔲 65E3

Museo Diocesano
✉ Piazza del Duomo 1
☎ 0575/62 830
🕐 Apr–end Sep Tue–Sun
   10–7; Oct–end Mar
   Tue–Sun 10–6
♿ Few
👊 Moderate

Museo dell'Accademia Etrusca
✉ Palazzo Casali, Piazza
   Signorelli 19
☎ 0575/630 415 or 637 235
🕐 Apr–end Oct Tue–Sun
   10–7; Nov–end Mar
   Tue–Sun 10–6
♿ Few
👊 Moderate

ℹ Tourist office: Via
   Nazionale 42
   (☎ 0575/630 352;
   www.cortona.net)

A view over the medieval rooftops of Cortona

Lucca

Lucca is one of Tuscany's gems, an immediately likable place of cobbled streets, tiny Romanesque churches, bristling towers and lovely medieval buildings: the sort of place, in the words of Henry James, 'overflowing with everything that makes for ease, for plenty, for beauty, for interest and good example' (*Italian Hours*, 1909). The town began life as a Roman colony, later becoming Tuscany's first Christian town and the seat of the region's Imperial rulers (the Margraves). Its medieval wealth was second only to Florence, thanks to its banking and textiles, allowing it to dominate western Tuscany for centuries. Independent until 1799, it passed to Napoleon in 1809 (the town was ruled by his sister, Elisa Baciocchi) and then to the Grand Duchy of Tuscany in 1847.

The bell tower of Lucca's ancient cathedral dates from 1070

🛈 Tourist offices: Piazzale Giuseppe Verdi (☎ 0583/442 944 or 0583/583 150; www.comune.lucca.it); Viale Luporini (☎ 0583/583 462; Apr–end Sep)

➕ 64B5

Giardino Botanico
✉ Via dell'Orto Botanico 14
☎ 0583/442 160
🕐 Jul–mid-Sep Mon–Sat 10–7; May, Jun Mon–Sat 10–6; mid- Mar to end Apr, mid-Sep–end Oct Mon–Fri 10–5; Nov–mid-Mar Mon–Fri 9.30–12.30, by appointment only
♿ Good 💶 Inexpensive

Walking Lucca's streets is a pleasure in itself, but no trip to the city would be complete without wandering part of the city walls, 4km (2.5 miles) in all, built in the 16th and 17th centuries as a defence against the Tuscan dukes. From their tree-lined ramparts you can enjoy panoramas over the pantiled rooftops, occasionally descending to explore sights such as the peaceful little **Giardino Botanico** (Botanic Gardens), in the city's southeast corner.

What to See in Lucca

DUOMO DI SAN MARTINO ✪✪✪

Lucca's cathedral is one of Tuscany's architectural master-pieces. The asymmetrical façade, begun in 1070, is famous for its carved reliefs, especially those over the central door—the *Life of St. Martin* and *Labours of the Months*—and those of the left portal (1233), probably by Nicola Pisano. Matteo Civitali (1435–1501), local sculptor, took charge inside, where he was responsible for the inlaid pavement, pulpit, water stoups, two tombs in the south transept and the vast *Tempietto* (midway down the nave), built to house the *Volto Santo*, a 'true effigy' of Christ carved after the Crucifixion (probably a 13th-century fake). This statue, which is robed rather than naked, in the Byzantine style, is carried through the streets of Lucca on the eve of the Feast of the Holy Cross (13 September). The interior's highlight is Jacopo della Quercia's *Tomb of Illaria del Carretto* (1410), one of Italy's most beautiful tombs (it is currently housed off the right nave: there is a small admission charge to view it). The cathedral also contains paintings by Fra Bartolomeo, Bronzino, Tintoretto and Domenico Ghirlandaio. Nearby the **Museo della Cattedrale** has a collection of religious and other objects.

MUSEO NAZIONALE DI VILLA GUINIGI ✪✪

The Museo Nazionale di Villa Guinigi, at the eastern end of the town, has a major collection of sculpture; paintings; and archaeological fragments, including objects dating back to the Etruscan and Roman periods. Among the exhibits are works by Jacopo della Quercia, Matteo Civitali, Fra Bartolomeo and paintings by anonymous Sienese and Lucchese masters. More paintings can be seen across the city in the **Pinacoteca Nazionale**, housed in the Palazzo Mansi, a wonderful rococo palace.

➕ 64B5
Duomo
✉ Piazza San Martino
🕐 Apr–end Oct daily 7–7; Nov–end Mar 7–5

Museo della Cattedrale
✉ Piazza Antelminelli
☎ 0583/490 530
🕐 Apr–end Oct daily 10–6; Nov–end Mar 10–2
♿ Few 💧 Moderate. Joint ticket with Church of San Giovanni and *Carretto* tomb

➕ 64B5
Museo Nazionale di Villa Guinigi
✉ Via della Quarquonia
☎ 0583/496 033
🕐 Tue–Sat 8.30–7.30, Sun 8.30–1.30.
♿ Good 💧 Moderate or expensive with joint ticket with Pinacoteca Nazionale di Palazzo Mansi

Pinacoteca Nazionale di Pallazzo Mansi
✉ Via Galli Tassi 43
☎ 0583/55 570 or 0583/583 461
🕐 Tue–Sat 8.30–7, Sun and public hols 8.30–1.
♿ Few 💧 Moderate or expensisve joint ticket with Villa Guinigi

🕂 64B5
✉ Piazza San Frediano
☎ None
🕐 Mon–Sat 8.30–12, 3–5, Sun 10.30–5 (except during services)
♿ Good: some steps
🎫 Free

Torre Guinigi
✉ Via Sant'Andrea 41
☎ 0583/48 524
🕐 May–end Aug daily 9am–11pm; Apr, Sep, Oct 9–9; Mar 9–7.30; Feb 9.30–6; Nov–end Dec 10–6; Jan 10–5. Closed 25 Dec
♿ Few
🎫 Moderate

San Frediano's façade mosaic depicts the Ascension with the Apostles below

SAN FREDIANO ⭐⭐

San Frediano (1112–47), the third of Lucca's major churches, is dominated by a superb 13th-century façade mosaic, while the dark interior features a wealth of sculptures and paintings. Pride of place goes to the magnificent *Fonta Lustrale*, a large and intricately carved 12th-century font. Behind it, a carved *Annunciation* by Andrea della Robbia is framed by festoons of terracotta fruit. Close by is the tomb of St. Zita, patron saint of serving maids. The Cappella Trenta (fourth chapel on the left) features two pavement tombs and a sculpted altarpiece (1422) by Jacopo della Quercia; the second chapel in the same aisle contains the city's best fresco cycle: Amico Aspertini's 16th-century scenes from the lives of San Frediano and St. Augustine as well as the *Arrival of the Volto Santo in Lucca* (see above). Just to the southeast of the church is Piazza Anfiteatro, an evocative square whose oval of crumbling houses mirrors the shape of the Roman amphitheatre which stood here until the 12th century. Many were partly built with stone from the amphitheatre.

A short distance south of Piazza Anfiteatro (walk via San Pietro Somaldi for its lovely façade) brings you to the Torre Guinigi, an eccentric city landmark built as a defensive tower by the Guinigi, one of Lucca's leading medieval families. A grove of ilex trees sprouts from its summit, and it has lovely views over the city.

SAN MICHELE IN FORO ✪✪✪

Lucca's streets focus on Piazza San Michele, site of the old Roman forum (*foro*), and now home to San Michele, one of Italy's loveliest churches. Some 300 years in the making, its façade is a wonderful confection of pillars, arcades and tiny twisted columns. The interior, by contrast, is plain, apart from a della Robbia terracotta and Filippino Lippi's *Saints Jerome, Sebastian, Roch and Helena*. West of the square lies the **Casa Natale di Puccini**, birthplace of Giacomo Puccini (1858–1924), and now a museum of memorabilia. To the east, San Cristoforo's walls are engraved with the names of Lucca's war dead.

The pillars, arcades and tiny columns of San Michele in Foro

➕ 64B5
Casa Natale di Puccini
✉ Via di Poggio, Corte San Lorenzo 8
☎ 0583/584 028
🕐 Daily 7.40–12, 3–6
Closed 1 Jan, 25 Dec
♿ Few
💰 Expensive
❓ Guided tours only

🕂 65D3

Fortezza

✉ Piazzale della Fortezza

☎ 0577/849 211

🕐 Apr–end Oct daily 9–8;
Nov–end Mar Tue–Sun
9–6

🍴 Wine and snacks from
the *enoteca* (€)

ℹ Tourist office: Costa del
Municipio 8, off Piazza
del Popolo (☎ 0577/849
331; www.
prolocomontalcino.it)

♿ Few

✋ Castle and *enoteca*: free.
Tower: moderate; joint
ticket with Museo Civico

Museo Civico

✉ Via Ricasoli 31

☎ 0577/846 014

🕐 Tue–Sun 10–1, 2–5.50
(5.40 Sep–end Mar)

🍴 Nearby (€)

♿ Good

✋ Moderate

Sant'Antimo

✉ 1km (.5 miles) from
Castelnuovo dell'Abate

☎ 0577/835 659

🕐 Mon–Sat 10.30–12.30,
3–6.30, Sun 9–10.30am

🍴 Nearby in Castelnuovo
dell'Abate (€)

♿ Good

✋ Free

MONTALCINO

Lofty Montalcino is one of Tuscany's most pleasing hill towns, with picture-perfect streets, magnificent views and some of the best wine in Italy (many shops sell the ubiquitous *Brunello* and *Rosso di Montalcino*). A fairy-tale **fortezza** (fortress) dominates the town's southern approaches, begun in 1361 and strengthened by Cosimo I in 1571 after the town had fallen to the Medici (Montalcino was the last town of the Sienese Republic to surrender to Florence). Inside is a little *enoteca* (wine bar) where you can sample local wines, along with a watchtower and battlements, with far-reaching views.

You can also buy wines at the Fiaschetteria Italiana, a pretty, turn-of-the-century café in Piazza del Popolo, the town's modest main square. On one side of the square stands the narrow Palazzo dei Priori (1292), on another the graceful arches of a Renaissance loggia. The town's new **Museo Civico** is housed in a monastery annexed to the fresco-filled church of Sant'Agostino. The museum is full of valuable wooden sculptures and wonderful Gothic and Renaissance paintings.

A few kilometres south of Montalcino lies **Sant'Antimo**, a superb Cistercian abbey beautifully situated in glorious pastoral countryside and reputedly founded by Charlemagne in 832, though most of the present Romanesque building dates from the 12th century. The stunning interior features several finely carved capitals: look for the second column on the right, where the capital shows *Daniel in the Lion's Den*. The ambulatory and its radiating chapels, unusual in Italian churches, were based on French models.

Montalcino's lovely Fiaschetteria Italiana is the perfect place to take time out from sightseeing

MONTEPULCIANO ✪✪

Ancient Montepulciano is the highest of the Tuscan hill towns, gazing down from its windblown eyrie across Lake Trasimeno and Umbria's hazy hills. Strung along a narrow ridge, the town hinges around a single main street—the Corso—a precipitous climb which passes a succession of interesting churches and Renaissance palaces. Look out for the Palazzo Cocconi (No 70), attributed to Antonio Sangallo; Vignola's Palazzo Tarugi (No 82); and the unmistakable Palazzo Bucelli (No 73), whose lower walls are studded with ancient Etruscan funerary urns.

Further up the hill you pass Sant'Agostino, designed by Michelozzo, the Medici's best-loved architect, and short detours take you to another pair of worthwhile churches: Santa Lucia and San Francesco. Pop in to the **Museo Civico**, home to a selection of Gothic and Renaissance works, and then recover your breath in the Piazza Grande, the town's main square. Here, the Palazzo Comunale's **tower** provides good views, while at Palazzo Cantucci, you can buy the town's famous red wine, *Vino Nobile di Montepulciano*.

Also here is the Duomo, whose high altar shelters Taddeo di Bartolo's radiant *Assumption* (1401) as well as fragments of Michelozzo's *Tomb of Bartolomeo Aragazzi* (1427–36). The baptistery chapel (first on the left) features a font and six bas-reliefs (1340) by Giovanni d'Agostino as well as a della Robbia terracotta which frames a relief of the *Madonna and Child* attributed to Benedetto da Maiano.

Finally, leave time for the ten-minute walk southwest, beyond the town walls, to **San Biagio**, a celebrated Renaissance church (1518–45) designed by Antonio Sangallo the Elder. The intention was that the church should house a miracle-producing image of the Madonna.

✚ 65E3

ℹ Tourist office: Piazzale Don Minzoni (☎ 0578/747 341; www.prolocomontepulciano.it/ www.comune.montepulciano.si.it)

Museo Civico

✉ Via Ricci 10

☎ 0578/717 300

🕐 Apr–end Oct Tue–Sun 10–1, 3–6; Nov–end Mar Tue–Sat 11–12.30, 3.30–4.30, Sun 10–1, 3–6

🍴 Nearby in Piazza Grande (€)

♿ Few 💰 Moderate

Torre Comunale

✉ Palazzo Comunale, Piazza Grande 1

☎ 0578/757 442 or 757 034

🕐 Call for times

🍴 Nearby in Piazza Grande (€)

♿ None 💰 Inexpensive

San Biagio

✉ Via di San Biagio 14

☎ None

🕐 Daily 9–12, 3–6

🍴 Overlooking church (€)

♿ Good 💰 Free

Hilltop Montepulciano

Piazza Pio II, heart of Pienza, a 'planned' Renaissance village

✚ 65E3
ℹ Tourist office: Piazza Pio II; ☎ 0578/749 071; www.comunedipienza.it

Duomo

✉ Piazza Pio II
☎ 0578/749 071
🕐 Daily 8–1, 3–7
🍴 Nearby in Piazza Pio II (€)
♿ Good 🎫 Free

Palazzo Piccolomini

✉ Piazza Pio II
☎ 0578/748 503
🕐 Tue–Sun 10–12.30, 3–6. Closed mid–Nov to mid–Dec
🍴 Nearby in Piazza Pio II (€)
♿ Poor 🎫 Inexpensive

Museo Diocesano di Pienza

✉ Corso Il Rossellino 30
☎ 0578/748 379
🕐 Mid-Mar to end Oct Wed–Mon 10–1, 2–6.30; Nov–mid-Mar Sat–Sun 10–1, 3–6
🍴 Nearby (€)
♿ Good 🎫 Moderate

PIENZA ✪✪

Pienza owes much of its present appearance to Aeneas Piccolomini, later Pope Pius II, who tried to turn the village—his birthplace—into a model Renaissance town. The transformation began in 1459, a year after he became pope, and was overseen by Bernardo Rossellino, one of the era's leading architects. Pius died before his dream was realized, and only the cathedral, a papal lodging and a handful of palaces were ever built.

Piazza Pio II is the heart of the planned extravagance, dominated by the classically inspired façade of the **Duomo** (note Pius's garlanded coat of arms in the upper pediment). The lofty interior—now showing alarming signs of collapse—was inspired by German 'hall churches' Pius had seen on his travels around Europe. The tall windows—another papal whim—were designed to create a flood of light, symbolizing the enlightenment of the age. Pius also commissioned the five beautiful Sienese altarpieces ranged around the walls.

To the right is the **Palazzo Piccolomini**, Pius's palace, with its glorious triple-tiered loggia and gardens providing some breathtaking views. Some rooms are open to the public, notably the papal bedroom and weapon-filled Sala d'Armi. Down the Corso Il Rossellino, just past the Piazza Pio II, is the **Museo Diocesano di Pienza**. It has a beautifully displayed collection of tapestries, manuscripts, silverware and Sienese paintings. The 14th-century papal cope is an outstanding example of English embroidery.

Don't miss the Pieve di Corsignano, an ancient parish church five minutes' walk from Pienza.

PISA ⚫⚫

Pisa has far more to offer than its famous leaning tower (▶ 25), not least the ensemble of sights on Piazza dei Miracoli, the broad grassy square that encloses not only the tower but also the town's cathedral, Baptistery and Camposanto. Begun in 1152, the **Baptistery** (Italy's largest) is a mixture of Romanesque and Gothic, the latter added by Nicola and Giovanni Pisano between 1270 and 1290. Nicola also carved the exceptional pulpit (1260); the interior is otherwise bare, except for a fine octagonal font (1246) by Guido da Como.

The **cathedral** is earlier, dating from 1063, though most of the interior was remodelled after a disastrous fire in 1595. Among the survivors of the conflagration were the bronze doors (1180) and Giovanni Pisano's majestic pulpit. The piazza's third component, the marble-walled **Camposanto**, is a medieval cemetery whose once famous frescoes were all but obliterated by Allied bombing in 1944. Its tombs and fragments, however, are still worth a visit.

Bombing destroyed much else in Pisa, but spared the exhibits of the **Museo dell'Opera del Duomo**, a 23-room museum with an uneven collection of paintings, sculptures and other objects. The **Museo Nazionale di San Matteo**, Pisa's main civic museum, is similarly hit-and-miss, but includes works by Masaccio, Donatello and Simone Martini. The town's loveliest church is Santa Maria della Spina, named after a spine (*spina*) from Christ's Crown of Thorns kept inside.

➕ 64B5

ℹ️ Tourist office: Piazza della Stazione 11 and Piazza del Duomo (☎ 050/560 464, 542 291, 541 800 or 542 344; www. pisa.turismo.toscana.it)

Duomo, Baptistery, Camposanto and Museo dell'Opera

✉️ Campo (Piazza) dei Miracoli

☎ 050/560 547 (all sights)

🕐 Duomo: Apr–end Sep Mon–Sat 8–7.30, Sun 1–7.30; Mar, Oct Mon–Sat 10–5.30; Nov–end Feb Mon–Sat 10–12.45, 3–4.30, Sun 3–4.30. Baptistery and Camposanto: Apr–end Oct daily 8–7.30; Mar, Oct 9–5.30; Jan–end Feb, Nov–end Dec 9–4.30. Museo dell'Opera: Apr–end Sep daily 8–7.20; Mar, Oct 9–5.20; Nov–end Feb 9–4.20

🍴 Nearby (€)

♿ Duomo, Baptistery and Camposanto: good. Museo dell'Opera del Duomo: few

🎫 Moderate (all sights); also a variety of combined tickets to a combination of sights

Museo Nazionale di San Matteo

✉️ Lungarno Mediceo

☎ 050/541 865

🕐 Tue–Sat 8.30–7, Sun 8.30–1

🍴 Nearby (€)

♿ Good

🎫 Moderate

Exchanging views in front of Pisa's magnificent cathedral

64C5

Tourist office: Palazzo dei Vescovi, Piazza del Duomo 4 (☎ 0573/21 622; www. comune.pistoia.it)

Cathedral

Piazza del Duomo

☎ 0573/25 095

Daily 8–12.30, 4–7

Cathedral: free. St. James Altar: inexpensive

Museo Civico

Palazzo del Comune, Piazza del Duomo

☎ 0573/3711 or 0573/371 214

Apr–end Oct Tue–Sat 10–6, Sun 9.30–12.30; Nov–end Feb Tue–Sat 10–5, Sun 9.30–12.30

Inexpensive

Pistoia's historic heart is filled with numerous appealing monuments such as this timeworn Renaissance well

PISTOIA ✪

Pistoia's industrial outskirts deter most visitors, which is a shame, for the town boasts a medieval centre and a group of churches and monuments that stand comparison with any in Tuscany. Piazza del Duomo, its captivating main square, is home to the Campanile, a former Lombard watchtower; several medieval palaces; a 14th-century baptistery; and the arched façade of the town's **cathedral**.

The last contains a font by Benedetto da Maiano (entrance wall) and the tomb of Cino da Pistoia (1337), writer and friend of Dante. The chief highlight is the St. James Altar (1287–1456), Italy's finest piece of medieval silverware. Weighing over a tonne, the work contains some 628 figures and depicts episodes from the Old and New Testaments. To the left and rear of the cathedral lies the **Museo Civico**, with a collection of paintings and sculptures.

Elsewhere in the town be sure to see the 12th-century church of San Bartolomeo in Pantano, which has a pulpit (1250) by Guido da Como; San Giovanni Fuorcivitas, known for its pulpit by Guglielmo da Pisa (1270); and Sant'Andrea, also famous for its pulpit (1301), an outstanding work by Giovanni Pisano. Sculpture of a different kind adorns the façade of the Ospedale del Ceppo, a 13th-century hospital decorated with a colourful glazed terracotta frieze (1514–25) by Giovanni della Robbia (*The Seven Works of Mercy*). Finally, visit the Cappella del Tau, a deconsecrated church noted for its 14th-century Gothic frescoes.

Chianti Drive

Leave Siena (➤ 85–90) to the north, picking up the N222 towards Castellina in Chianti (21km/13 miles). From Castellina take the N429 east to Radda in Chianti (10km/6 miles). Two kilometres (1mile) or so east of Radda at Villa there is an optional scenic circuit to the north (15km/9 miles), via Volpaia. Return to the main road at Villa.

The N222 is one of the more scenic roads in Chianti, but like many in the region it is fairly twisting, so distances are often a good deal longer than they appear on the map. Both Castellina and Radda are major wine producers, and both have pretty central cores, but their outskirts have been tarnished by new building. Volpaia has an evocative 16th-century castle and several watchtowers.

From Radda head east to Badia a Coltibuono (6km/4 miles) and then drive south on the N408 to Gaiole in Chianti (5km/3 miles). South of the village (3km/2 miles), turn left and follow a lovely minor road past Castagnoli, Linari and San Gusmé (20km/12 miles). Turn right on the N484 to Castello di Brolio (8km/5 miles).

Badia is part of an abbey complex owned by one of Chianti's leading producers. You can eat in the restaurant here (see the panel opposite for details) or buy wine, honey and virgin olive oil from the estate shop. Gaiole is an unexceptional village, but the Castello di Brolio is more appealing: One of Chianti's oldest vineyards, it has been owned by the Ricasoli family since 1167. Wine can be bought here also, and there are occasional organized tours of the winery.

Chianti is best known for its famous red wines

From Brolio return to Siena (26km/16 miles) on the N408 via San Giovanni.

Distance
110km (68 miles) depending on optional detours

Time
Allow a day

Start/end point
Siena
✚ 65D3

Lunch
Restaurant (€€)
✉ Badia a Coltibuono
☎ 0577/749424;
www.coltibuono.com
🕐 Closed Jan to mid-Mar and Mon Nov–end Apr

San Gimignano

Tuscany's most famous village is a picture of medieval perfection, its famous towers rising above orange-tiled houses and atmospheric streets. Two superb churches, swathed with frescoes, add to its charm; only the summer immense crowds detract from the village's appeal. An Etruscan and then a Roman settlement, it enjoyed its heyday during the Middle Ages, when its position, close to trade and pilgrimage routes, brought great prosperity. Family rivalries and the Black Death brought its eventual downfall, and in 1348 the village surrendered itself to the protection of Florence. Thereafter it became a sleepy backwater until the arrival of tourism this century.

San Gimignano's famous skyline has been likened to a 'medieval Manhattan'

 64C4

ℹ️ Tourist Office:
Piazza del Duomo 1
(☎ 0577/940 008;
www.sangimignano.com)

A combined San Gimignano ticket gives admission to the Museo Civico, Torre Grossa, Cappella di Santa Fina (Collegiata), Museo Archeologico-Spezieria di Santa Fina and Museo Ornitologico (a museum of stuffed birds south of the Rocca).

What to See in San Gimignano

COLLEGIATA (▶ 18, TOP TEN)

MUSEO D'ARTE SACRA   ✪

An arch to the left of the Collegiata leads to San Gimignano's Baptistery, whose loggia is frescoed with an *Annunciation* (1482) by Ghirlandaio and Sebastiano Mainardi. The courtyard here contains the entrance to the Museo d'Arte Sacra, a modest museum with Etruscan remains, a *Madonna and Child* by Bartolo de Fredi, an early wooden Crucifix, exquisite illuminated choir books, and a marble bust of Onofrio di Pietro (1493), a local scholar, by Benedetto da Maiano.

➕ 64C4
✉️ Piazza Pecori
☎ 0577/940 316
🕐 Apr–end Oct Mon–Fri 9.30–7.30, Sat 9.30–5, Sun 1–5; Mar and Oct–mid-Jan Mon–Sat 9.30–5, Sun 1–5
🍴 Nearby (€) ♿ Few
👆 Inexpensive. Admission also by combined ticket

MUSEO CIVICO/TORRE GROSSA ★★★

San Gimignano's principal museum is entered through a lovely courtyard, with a loggia partly covered in frescoes by Sodoma and Taddeo di Bartolo. After climbing the stairs you can either enter the museum or climb the Torre Grossa, the only village tower open to the public.

The museum's first room (downstairs) is the frescoed Sala di Dante, so-called because the poet spoke here in 1300 during a diplomatic mission from Florence. Its highlight is Lippo Memmi's eye-catching *Maestà* (1317). Stairs lead to the picture gallery with a large salon and several smaller rooms on the right and one tiny stone-walled room to the left. Enter this first to see three quaint frescoes (1320) showing a husband and wife playing and taking a shared bath before climbing into bed.

In the other rooms are outstanding paintings by Filippino Lippi, Pintoricchio and Benozzo Gozzoli as well as several vivid polyptychs describing the lives of saints Fina and San Gimignano (two of the village patron saints). Look, too, for a crucifixion by Coppo di Marcovaldo.

➕ 64C4
✉ Piazza del Duomo
☎ 0577/990 348
🕐 Tower and museum: Mar–end Oct daily 9.30–7.30; Nov–end Feb 10–5.30,
🍴 Nearby (€)
♿ Few
🏛 Museum: moderate. Tower: moderate. Combined museum-tower ticket: expensive

Enjoy a drink in Piazza della Cisterna after exploring San Gimignano

🕀 64C4

Sant'Agostino

✉ Piazza Sant'Agostino
☎ None
🕐 Apr–end Oct daily 7.30–12, 3–7; Nov–end Mar 7.30–12, 3–6
🍴 Nearby (€)
♿ Good: some steps
🎫 Free

Museo Archeologico

✉ Via Folgore 11
☎ 0577/940 348
🕐 Apr–end Oct Sat–Thu 11–6; Nov–end Dec Sat–Thu 10–2
♿ Good
🎫 Moderate

PIAZZA DELLA CISTERNA ✪✪

Most people approach central San Gimignano from Porta San Giovanni in the south. From here Via San Giovanni leads past San Francesco, a deconsecrated Pisan-Romanesque church which now serves as a *cantina* selling the village's celebrated white wine (► 42–43). Be sure to walk to the lovely little garden at the back for superb views. At the end of the street you enter Piazza della Cisterna, one of the village's two linked main squares (the other is Piazza del Duomo). The piazza takes its name from the public cistern (1273) which sits at its heart, though the square is more noteworthy for the various medieval palaces and towers on all sides.

ROCCA ✪

A short walk from Piazza del Duomo takes you to the Rocca, San Gimignano's old fortress, built in 1353 on the orders of the Florentines. Two centuries later another Florentine, Cosimo I, ordered its destruction (just one of the original towers survives). Today the ruins enclose a pleasant little park with sweeping views from the old ramparts.

SANT'AGOSTINO ✪✪

The church of Sant'Agostino, begun in 1298, is best known for Benozzo Gozzoli's chancel frescoes of scenes from the *Life of St. Augustine* (1463–7). The striking high altar painting, the *Coronation of the Virgin* (1483), is the work of Piero del Pollaiolo; the frescoes on the *Life of the Virgin* (1356) on the walls of the chapel right of the high altar are by Bartolo di Fredi.

The rear wall contains the Cappella di San Bartolo (on the left as you enter), celebrated for its magnificent altar (1495) by Benedetto da Maiano. Its reliefs depict three miracles by San Bartolo, one of the village patron saints, who is buried in the chapel. The three figures above portray the Theological Virtues; Sebastiano Mainardi's frescoes, to the left, show saints Lucy, Nicholas of Bari and Gimignano, the last holding the town of San Gimignano in his arms. The four half-figures (1318) on the church's left wall, by Mino da Fiesole, are believed to be part of Bartolo's original shrine. On the right (south) wall are several notable frescoes, including a *Madonna and Child with Eight Saints* (1494) by Pier Francesco Fiorentino and *Christ with the Symbols of the Passion* by Bartolo di Fredi.

Just south of the church in the old Santa Fina convent is the **Museo Archeologico**, with Roman and Etrusan finds and the Spezieria di Santa Fina, a medieval pharmacy.

Southern Tuscany Drive

Leave San Gimignano (➤ 80–82) and drive on minor roads southeast to Colle di Val d'Elsa (14km/9 miles). Continue to Monteriggioni (9km/6miles) before meeting the Florence– Siena superstrada. Follow this to Siena (➤ 85–90), then take the city's ring road south before picking up the N326 (22km/14 miles) for Sinalunga.

Colle di Val d'Elsa is unattractive on its outskirts but retains a beguiling medieval centre with the Duomo, San Francesco and a clutch of smaller churches and museums all worth seeing. Unmissable Monteriggioni is a perfect village, with a couple of streets, old walls and towers.

Follow the N326 briefly before turning right (south) on the minor N438 to Asciano (20km/12 miles). From Asciano take minor lanes south to Monte Oliveto Maggiore (9km/6 miles), then continue to Buonconvento (9km/6 miles) and south to Montalcino (14km/ 9 miles) and Sant'Antimo (10km/6 miles, ➤ 74).

Distance
160km (99 miles)

Time
1–2 days depending on stops

Start point
San Gimignano
✠ 64C4

End point
Montepulciano
✠ 65E3

Lunch
Taverna Grappolo Blu (€–€€)
✉ Via Scala di Moglio 1, off Via Mazzini
☎ 0577/847 150

Classic Tuscan countryside near San Quirico d'Orcia

The road to Asciano takes you through the *crete*, the Sienese 'badlands', a region of bare clay hills and distant views. Stop at the abbey of Monte Oliveto, famous for its fresco cycles by Sodoma and Luca Signorelli.

From Sant'Antimo take minor roads east towards the main N2 (21km/13 miles) past the village of Castiglione d'Orcia. Turn left on the N2 and detour briefly to Bagno Vignoni (2km/1 mile), known for the old spa pool in its main square. Then visit the famous Romanesque Collegiata at San Quirico d'Orcia (6km/4 miles) before picking up the N146 east to Pienza (10km/6 miles, ➤ 76) and Montepulciano (13km/8 miles, ➤ 75).

🛈 Tourist offices:
Colle di Val d'Elsa Via Campana 43 (☎ 0577/922 791 (closed Feb and am Nov–end Mar).
Asciano Corso Matteotti 18 (☎ 0577/719 510 or 718 745 summer only).
San Quirico d'Orcia Via Dante Alighieri 33 (☎ 0577/897 211 summer only)

Siena

Siena is Italy's loveliest medieval city. Originally Etruscan, it became a Roman colony and later the capital of a medieval republic and the principal rival to Florence. Italy's finest piazza, the Campo, forms its heart, providing the stage for the Palio, a famous annual horse race. Here, too, is the Palazzo Pubblico, home to some of the city's greatest works of art. Nearby lie the treasure-filled Duomo, one of Italy's greatest Gothic buildings, and the Ospedale di Santa Maria della Scala, which houses two outstanding fresco cycles. Alongside the Duomo, the Museo dell'Opera shelters the most majestic of all Siena's paintings, Duccio's multi-panelled *Maestà*.

➕ 65D3
ℹ️ Tourist office: Piazza del Campo 56
(☎ 0577/280551; www.terresiena.it)
🕐 Summer: Mon–Sat 8:30–7.30, Sun 9–3; winter: Mon–Fri 8.30–6.30, Sat 8.30–1, Sun 9–3

What to See in Siena

CAMPO, PIAZZA DEL (▶ 16, TOP TEN)
DUOMO (▶ 20, TOP TEN)

MUSEO DELL'OPERA DEL DUOMO   ✪✪✪

This museum occupies part of a half-finished extension to the cathedral, which would have made it the largest church in Italy (work was abandoned following the Black Death in 1348). It opens with the Gallerie delle Statue, with a tondo by Donatello in the middle of the room, a *Madonna and Child* by Jacopo della Quercia (Siena's leading medieval sculptor) and a series of wall statues by Giovanni Pisano from the cathedral's façade. Upstairs, in a special room, stands Duccio's *Maestà* (1308–11), a magnificent work consisting of a vast main altarpiece and countless tiny panels. Other treats are the anonymous *Madonna dagli Occhi Grossi* (Madonna of the Large Eyes) and the view from the tower.

Exhibits in the Museo dell'Opera del Duomo

www.operaduomo.it
➕ 86B2
✉️ Piazza de Duomo 8
☎ 0577/283 048;
🕐 Mid-Mar–end Sep daily 9–7.30; Oct 9–6;Jan to mid-Mar and Nov–end Dec 9–1.30
🍴 Nearby (€)
♿ Good
💰 Expensive

www.santamaria.comune.
siena.it
86B1
Piazza del Duomo 2
0577/586 410;
Mid-Mar–end Oct daily
10.30–6.30; Nov–mid-Mar
10.30–4.30
Shop and café (€)
Very good
Expensive

OSPEDALE DI SANTA MARIA DELLA SCALA ✪✪

For almost 800 years this large building opposite the Duomo served as an orphanage and hospital. Following its recent closure there are plans to turn it into a vast cultural centre. More and more of the medieval complex is being opened to the public, revealing superlative works of art hidden from view for centuries. Chief of these is a vast fresco cycle (1444) by Domenico di Bartolo and Vecchietta, whose perfectly preserved panels decorate what until recently was a large hospital ward. The pictures show the foundation and daily life of the medieval hospital. A smaller stone-vaulted chapel, the Sagrestia Vecchia, is decorated with another fresco cycle by Vecchietta, who sculpted the famous high altar statue of the *Risen Christ* in SS. Annunziata, the hospital's former church. In the bowels of the building lies the eerie Oratorio di Santa Caterina della Notte where St. Catherine once passed nocturnal vigils.

Siena is full of atmospheric little side streets

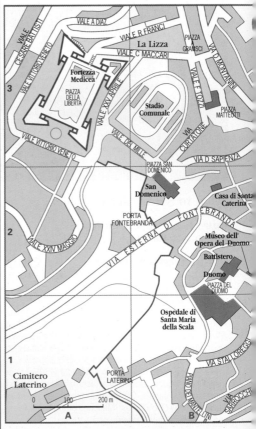

PALAZZO PUBBLICO

OOO

The Palazzo Pubblico's medieval outline dominates the Campo's southern flank. Begun in 1297, it was designed as civic offices and still houses various council departments. From its courtyard an entrance (on the left) leads to the **Torre del Mangia** (102m/632ft), reputedly named after its first bell-ringer, a wastrel whose nickname—the *Mangiaguadagni*—meant 'the eater of profits'. The views from the summit are breathtaking. A door to the right of the courtyard leads to the **Museo Civico**, a series of chambers decorated by Siena's leading medieval and Renaissance artists. Some of the city's most famous paintings are here, including Simone Martini's exquisite *Maestà* (1315–21) and the series of paintings by Ambrogio Lorenzetti on *Good and Bad Government* (1338). Look out for the equestrian portrait of *Guidoriccio da Fogliano*, opposite the *Maestà*, controversially attributed to Martini.

✚ 87C2

Torre del Mangia
✉ Piazza del Campo 1
☎ 0577/292 296
🕑 Mid-Mar to end Oct daily 10–7; Nov–mid-Mar 10–4
🍴 Nearby in Piazza del Campo (€–€€)
♿ Few
💶 Expensive
❓ The tower has 503 steps

Museo Civico
✉ Piazza del Campo 1
☎ 0577/292 296
🕑 Mid-Mar to end Oct daily 10–7; Nov and mid-Feb to mid-Mar 10–6.30; Dec–mid-Feb 10–5.30
🍴 Nearby in Piazza del Campo (€–€€)
♿ Good
💶 Expensive

SIENA

✚ 87C1
✉ Palazzo Buonsignori, Via San Pietro 29
☎ 0577/270 508
🕐 Mon 8.30–1.30, Tue–Sat 8.15–7.15, Sun 8.15–1.15
🍴 Nearby (€)
♿ Good
👆 Moderate

PINACOTECA NAZIONALE

Siena's Pinacoteca is one of Italy's finest art galleries, its warren of rooms tracing the development of Sienese painting over some 500 years. A lovely and distinct school, the Sienese painters—notably Duccio—drew their early inspiration from Byzantine art, revelling in gold backgrounds, sumptuous tones and stylized Madonnas. Later artists—Pietro Lorenzetti and Simone Martini in particular—moulded these earlier styles to their own purpose, producing beautifully lyrical paintings whose influence was felt as far afield as England and the Netherlands. The gallery then deals with painters such as Sassetta and Giovanni di Paolo, who took stock of Florentine innovations, blending the traditional Sienese motifs with the new wave of Renaissance thinking. Finally the gallery touches on some of Siena's Mannerist stars.

✚ 87C1
✉ Prato di Sant'Agostino
☎ No tel
🕐 Apr–end Oct daily 10.30–1.30, 3–5.30; hours vary, consult tourist office
👆 Inexpensive

SANT'AGOSTINO

Begun in 1258, Sant'Agostino's interior was remodelled along Baroque lines by Vanvitelli some 500 years later. The church keeps very irregular hours, but is well worth visiting for a handful of outstanding paintings. Perugino's *Crucifixion* (1506) occupies the second altar of the right (south) aisle. Alongside it, the Cappella Piccolomini contains an *Adoration of the Magi* (1518) by Sodoma and a 14th-century lunette fresco of the *Madonna and Child with Saints* by Ambrogio Lorenzetti. The Cappella Bichi in the south transept has more frescoes and two monochrome medallions by Luca Signorelli.

✚ 86B2
✉ Piazza San Domenico
☎ No tel
🕐 Daily 9–12, 3–5
👆 Free

SAN DOMENICO

This vast Gothic church, begun by the Dominicans in 1226, is associated with St. Catherine of Siena, Italy's joint patron saint (with St. Francis). The Cappella delle Volte, right of the entrance, features a contemporary portrait (1414) of the saint, and the Cappella di Santa Caterina (midway down the right aisle) has frescoes of scenes from her life by Sodoma (1526). Her skull is kept in the chapel's altar tabernacle. Left of the chapel is a detached fresco of the *Madonna and Child* by Pietro Lorenzetti, brother of Ambrogio (both probably died in the plague of 1384). The first chapel to the right of the high altar houses Matteo di Giovanni's triptych of the *Madonna and Child with Saints*. Adorning the high altar are a tabernacle and sculpted angels (1475) by Benedetto da Maiano; the second chapel to its left has a *St. Barbara and Saints* (Matteo di Giovanni's masterpiece) and *Madonna and Child* by Benvenuto di Giovanni.

Right: Looking across the rooftops to San Domenico, a Gothic church begun in 1226

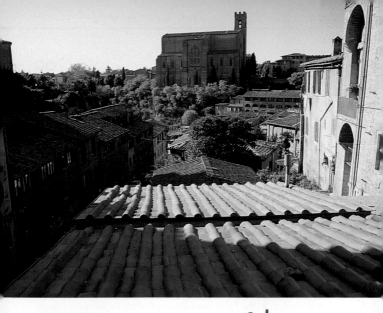

SAN FRANCESCO ⭐

A fire in 1655 left San Francesco stripped of all but a few works of art. Surviving fragments include a *Crucifixion* (1331) by Pietro Lorenzetti (first chapel left of high altar) and two graphic frescoes by Pietro and his brother Ambrogio (third chapel). The sacristy has a fine polyptych by Lippo Vanni of the *Madonna and Child with Four Saints* (1370), and at the end of the right (south) aisle is the 14th-century tomb of the Tolomei. Outside the church is the **Oratorio di San Bernardino**, whose beautifully panelled upper chapel has 14 large frescoes by Sodoma, Beccafumi and Girolamo del Pacchia (1496–1518).

✠ 87D3
✉ Piazza San Francesco
☎ Oratorio 0577/283 048
🕐 Church: daily 9–12, 3–5. Oratorio di San Bernardino: daily 10.30–1.30, 3–5.30
💰 Church: free. Oratorio: inexpensive
🍴 Nearby (€)
♿ Few

SANTA MARIA DEI SERVI ⭐⭐

This outlying church is worth the walk for its works of art and the lovely view of the city from its shady terrace. The first main altar on the right contains the *Madonna di Bordone* (1261) by Coppo di Marcovaldo, a Florentine artist; the last altar on the right features Matteo di Giovanni's *Massacre of the Innocents* (1491). An earlier version of the latter subject by Pietro Lorenzetti occupies the right wall of the second chapel right of the high altar. Other works include *The Adoration of the Shepherds* (1404) by one of Lorenzetti's followers, Taddeo di Bartolo; *Madonna della Misericordia* (1431) by one of Taddeo's pupils, Giovanni di Paolo; and *Madonna del Belvedere* (1363) by Jacopo di Mino.

✠ 87D1
☎ No tel
✉ Piazza Manzoni
🕐 Daily 9–12.30, 3–5
💰 Free

Did you know ?

Coppo di Marcovaldo was captured by the Sienese at the Battle of Montaperti in 1260 and forced to paint the Madonna in Santa Maria dei Servi as part of his ransom for release.

VOLTERRA ⊙⊙

A windblown Etruscan town, Volterra commands wide views across eerie grey-brown hills, many riddled with the deposits of alum and alabaster that have long been the region's economic mainstay. Learn more in the Alabaster Museum (Museo Storico dell'Alabastro). The main Piazza dei Priori is home to the Palazzo dei Priori (1208–57), known for Orcagna's painting of the *Annunciation* (1383) in the first-floor Sala del Consiglio. Also here is the Torre del Porcellino (Piglet's Tower), named after the carved boar to the right of the top window. Here, too, is the former Bishops' Palace, part of which is taken up with the **Museo d'Arte Sacra**, three rooms of paintings and sculpture.

Backing on to Piazza dei Priori is the Piazza del Duomo, site of a pretty Baptistery (currently closed for restoration) and the Duomo, celebrated for Mino da Fiesole's high altar tabernacle and sculpted angels (1471); an anonymous *Desposition* (chapel in the left transept); and a painted background by Benozzo Gozzoli to two terracotta figures by Zaccaria da Voltera (north aisle). A little way north lies the **Pinacoteca-Museo Civico**, renowned for Rosso Fiorentino's *Descent from the Cross* (1521), a Mannerist masterpiece, and earlier Sienese and Florentine paintings. Be sure to see the *balze*, Volterra's famous eroded cliffs; the Roman theatre and other sights in the town's Archaeolgocial Zone (to the north); and the wealth of Etruscan objects in the **Museo Etrusco Guarnacci**.

⊞ 64C4

Museo d'Arte Sacra
⊠ Via Roma 13
☎ 0588/86 290
🕐 Mid-Mar to mid-Oct daily 9–1, 3–6; mid-Oct to mid-Mar 9–1
💰 Expensive

Museo Etrusco Guarnacci
⊠ Via Don Minzoni 15
☎ 0588/86 347
🕐 Mid-Mar to end Oct daily 9–7; Nov–mid-Mar 9–2
💰 Expensive. Joint ticket with Pinacoteca

Pinacoteca-Museo Civico
⊠ Palazzo Minucci-Solaini, Via dei Sarti 1 (off Piazza dei Priori)
☎ 0588/87 580
🕐 Mid-Mar to end Oct daily 9–7; Nov–mid-Mar 8.30–1.30
💰 Expensive

❓ *Biglietto Unico* (a single ticket) is valid for the Museo Etrusco Guarnacci, Pinacoteca-Museo Civico and Teatro Romano-Archaeological Zone

ℹ Tourist Office: Piazza dei Priori 20 (☎ 0588/86 099; www.volterratur.it)

Volterra is well known for its range of Roman remains

Where To...

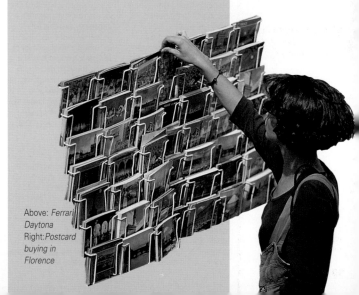

Above: Ferrari
Daytona
Right:Postcard
buying in
Florence

Florence

Prices

€   = under €30
€€   = €30–€50
€€€   = more than €50

Meals

The Florentine breakfast (*prima colazione*) is usually a simple stand-up affair of *cappuccino* and plain, cream- or jam-filled croissants (*brioche or cornetti*). Unless breakfast is included in your room rate it is always better and less expensive to take it in a bar. Lunch (*pranzo*) starts around 12.30pm, but is rarely the extended blow-out of days gone by—this might be the time to save money by buying a picnic from a market or local food shop (*un alimentare*). Dinner (*cena*) is served from around 8pm.

Florence East

Alle Muratte (€€)

Among the city's top-rated restaurants, and one of the first choices for a fairly-priced meal in surroundings which are welcoming and pleasant without being overly precious. The cooking is simple and assertive, revelling in innovative interpretations of traditional Tuscan and southern Italian dishes. There is also a little *Vineria* (wine bar) where you can enjoy a selection of dishes from the main menu at around half-price. Reserve ahead.

✉ Via Ghibellina 52–54r
☎ 055/240 618 🕐 Closed lunch, Mon & Aug 🚌 14, 23 & shuttle bus B

Baldovino (€€)

This stylish cozy restaurant in the shadow of Santa Croce is good by any standards. It is owned by a Scottish couple who also run the small wine bar opposite and the equally successful and appealing sister restaurants Francescano (almost next door) and the pricier, more austere Beccofino across the river at Piazza degli Scarletti 1r. You can eat pizzas at Baldovino or full meals from a menu (which changes monthly) of well-cooked Tuscan staples.

✉ Via San Giuseppe 2r
☎ 055/241 773 🕐 Closed Mon 🚌 13, 23 & shuttle bus B

Beccofino (€€)

A sister restaurant to Baldovino and just as good and popular. More modern and pared down in appearance with a wine bar to one side, airy dining room to the other. Creative Tuscan cooking is the norm.

✉ Pisazza degli Scarlatti 1r (off Lungarno Guicciardini)
☎ 055/290 076 🕐 Closed lunch & Mon

Cibreo (€€–€€€)

Most people rank this relaxed and well-known place just behind the Enoteca Pinchiorri in the roll call of Florentine restaurants. Prices here, however, are much lower. It is a touchstone of simple Tuscan cooking and has spawned a café and delicatessen as well as a less expensive, more hectic, bistro-type annexe at the rear of the restaurant, where you can eat in less relaxed surroundings.

✉ Via del Verrocchio 8-Via dei Macci 118r ☎ 055/234 1100 🕐 Closed Sun, Mon & Aug 🚌 6, 23

Da Ganino (€–€€)

Good places to eat close to the Duomo and central Via dei Calzaiuoli are hard to find. This simple and reasonably priced restaurant is an exception to the rule. It also has tables outside in a little square in the summer. If it is full try the adjacent Birreria Centrale.

✉ Piazza dei Cimatori 4r
☎ 055/214 125 🕐 Closed Sun 🚌 In the pedestrian zone: nearest services 1, 6, 7, 11, 14

Dino (€€)

Dino is one of the city's most venerable restaurants and over the years has served consistently good Tuscan food to generations of Florentines. Suitable for family outings and business lunches alike.

✉ Via Ghibellina 51r
☎ 055/241 452 🕐 Closed Sun evening & Mon lunch

Enotecca Pinchiorri (€€€)

There is no question that this is one of Florence's best (and most expensive) restaurants: many food writers place it among the top five in Italy. Its lovely 15th-century palazzo setting, food and wine cellar (over 80,000 bottles from across the world) are without rival, though the rarified atmosphere and ceremony associated with eating here may not be to all tastes. An eight-course *degustazione* menu is available. Jacket and tie recommended for men. Reservations are essential.

✉ **Via Ghibellina 87**
☎ **055/242 777** 🕐 **Closed Wed lunch, Mon, Sun & Aug**
🚌 **13, 23 & shuttle bus B**

Pallottino (€–€€)

This is one of the city's newer restaurants and in a short time has become one of its busiest and trendiest. The food suggests real skill in the kitchen. Service is of a high standard and the attention to detail impressive. Located just northwest of Piazza Santa Croce.

✉ **Via Isola delle Stinche 1r**
☎ **055/289 573** 🕐 **Closed Mon evening** 🚌 **13, 23 & shuttle bus B**

Paoli (€€)

The food here may not be the best in the city, but few Florentine restaurants are as old or as beautiful. Most people come here for the atmospheric vaulted and frescoed dining room: The location is also very central (take the street off Via dei Calzaiuoli opposite Orsanmichele). Reserve a table or arrive early to be sure of getting a seat.

✉ **Via dei Tavolini 12r** ☎ **055/216 215** 🕐 **Closed Tue**
🚌 **In the pedestrian zone: nearest services 1, 6, 7, 11, 14**

Florence North
Antellesi (€–€€)

This easygoing place is increasingly well-known, though its popularity has pushed prices up and put pressure on the formerly relaxed service. Simple wooden tables and traditional Tuscan dishes such as *ribollita* and *bistecca*. Close to the Cappelle Medicee. Arrive early to be sure of a table. Note that there are a handful of tables at the front of the restaurant and far more tucked away to the rear.

✉ **Via Faenza 9r** ☎ **055/216 990** 🕐 **Closed Sun** 🚌 **6, 11**

Don Chisciotte (€€)

Smaller than many Florentine restaurants (just 40 covers) and with three high-vaulted and tastefully appointed dining rooms. Much—but not all—of Don Chisciotte's menu is devoted to fish, together with some interesting seafood and pasta combinations. Located in a street off the west side of Piazza dell'Indipendenza (northeast of the station).

✉ **Via Cosimo Ridolfi 4r**
☎ **055/475 430** 🕐 **Closed Mon lunch, Sun & Aug** 🚌 **All services to the rail station**

Le Fonticine (€€)

This well-known and long-established family-run restaurant combines dishes from Tuscany and Emilia-Romagna. The rustic and self-conscious atmosphere suggests it has tourists in mind, but the traditional food, especially the home-made pastas, is perfectly acceptable. Try the wild boar (*cinghiale*) and tripe (*trippa*) if you are feeling adventurous.

✉ **Via Nazionale 79r**
☎ **055/282 106** 🕐 **Closed Sun, Mon & three weeks in Aug**
🚌 **All services to the rail station**

Menus

An Italian menu (*la lista*) begins with a list of starters (*antipasti*), followed by first courses (*primi or primi piatti*), the latter consisting of soups, pastas and risottos. The main course—meat or fish—is a *secondo*, with salad (*insalata*) and vegetables (*contorni*) served separately. Puddings (*dolci*), cheese (*formaggio*) and fruit (*frutta*) follow, often rounded off with coffee—Italians always have an *espresso, never* a cappuccino—liqueurs and *digestivi*. Bear in mind that few people wade through the entire menu, so in all but the smartest restaurants you can be happy with a pasta, salad and glass of wine. Italians often walk to a *gelateria* for an ice cream as an alternative to a restaurant pudding. When ordering expensive meats, in particular the famous *bifstecca alla fiorentina*, the dish is often priced by the *etto* (100g/approx 4oz): items thus priced are labelled *S.Q.* or *hg*.

Paying

The bill is *il conto*—at the end of the meal ask for *il conto, per favore*—and usually includes a cover charge per person known as *pane e coperto*, though this is increasingly frowned on and attempts are being made to make the charge illegal. Service (*servizio*) may also be added. Remember that bars and restaurants are required by law to give you a proper receipt (*una ricevuta*), so if you are unhappy with a semi-legible scrawl on a scrap of paper—still sometimes presented in inexpensive places—you are within your rights to ask for a proper itemised bill.

Sabatini (€€€)

This smart and historic restaurant was formerly one of Florence's most exalted dining places. The Italian-International food is now only intermittently outstanding though still remains good enough to satisfy more than its fair share of Florentines. Service and the choice of wines are both generally excellent.

📧 **Via Panzani 9a** ☎ **055/211 559** 🕔 **Closed Mon** 🚌 **14, 17, 23**

Taverna del Bronzino (€€)

This rarefied but unstuffy restaurant has been an address of note for years and a popular choice with business people and smart Florentines. The cooking is traditional Tuscan, the service efficient and courteous. Pastas are good, especially the *linguine al pesto* and *cappellacci al cedro*. Both meat and fish dishes are available. To find the restaurant take Via San Gallo north from the Cenacolo di Sant'Apollonia: Via delle Ruote is the first left.

📧 **Via delle Ruote 25r** ☎ **055/495 220** 🕔 **Closed Sun & Aug** 🚌 **1, 6, 7, 11 & other services to San Marco**

Florence West
Belle Donne (€–€€)

This tiny place, full of convivial shared tables, is eye-catchingly festooned with mountainous displays of fruit, flowers and vegetables. Good, wholesome Tuscan cooking, with daily menus chalked on a blackboard. The informal ambience makes this a better bet for lunch or an early evening snack than for a full dinner. Located just southeast of Piazza Santa Maria Novella.

📧 **Via delle Belle Donne 16r** ☎ **238 2609** 🕔 **Closed Aug** 🚌 **6, 9, 11**

Cantinetta Antinori (€€)

Owned by one of Tuscany's oldest and most famous wine dynasties, this elegant wine bar uses wines, cheese and oils from the family's extensive estates. The beautiful panelled dining salons form part of an 18th-century *palazzo*, though the tables are close packed and the service and ambience deliberately lively. A place for an upscale snack or light meal, but be sure to dress up.

📧 **Piazza Antinori 3** ☎ **055/292 234** 🕔 **Closed Sat, Sun** 🚌 **6, 11, 31, 37**

Coco Lezzone (€€)

A well-known and rather trendy restaurant with simple, communal tables where you mix with Florentines and fellow visitors. The white-tiled dining rooms date from the building's former role as a dairy. Cooking is rigorously Tuscan though prices, while relatively reasonable, are higher than the food deserves: you are paying here for atmosphere and 'authenticity'. You may also be expected to move on to make way for new diners.

📧 **Via del Parioncino 26, off Lungarno Corsini** ☎ **055/287 178** 🕔 **Closed Sun, last week of Jul & all of Aug** 🚌 **11, 31, 32, 36, 37**

Latini (€)

An inexpensive, cheerful and much-frequented *trattoria*, beloved of visitors and Florentines alike though the crowded tables and raucous atmosphere may not be to all tastes. Its popularity has recently seen a modest rise in prices and a slight fall in standards though the robust Tuscan food remains as good as ever.

✉ **Via dei Palchetti, off Via della Vigna Nuova** ☎ **055/210 916** ⓘ **Closed Mon** 🚍 **11, 31, 32, 36, 37**

Oliviero (€€)
A mixture of creative and conservative Florentine cooking that can range from the very good to the sublime: on its day this is one of the city's very best restaurants. This said, the service and kitchen output can sometimes be a little erratic.

✉ **Via delle Terme 51r** ☎ **055/212 421** ⓘ **Closed lunch, Mon & Aug** 🚍 **11, 31, 32, 36, 37**

Zà-Zà (€€)
Zà-Zà has been serving the central market's traders and customers for over 20 years, offering set-price meals (usually a choice of several pastas and three or four main courses) in an inviting brick-arched and stone-walled interior. It has become better known, thanks to some high-profile celebrity customers, and prices have crept up. Reserve in summer.

✉ **Piazza del Mercato Centrale 26r** ☎ **055/215 411** ⓘ **Closed Sun & part of Aug** 🚍 **On the edge of pedestrian zone**

Florence Oltrarno
Angiolino (€–€€)
Food here can be slightly erratic, but this is a pretty and also reasonably priced restaurant that remains true to its Florentine culinary roots. The varied *antipasti* are particularly good.

✉ **Via Santo Spirito 36r** ☎ **055/239 8976** ⓘ **Closed late Jul–mid-Aug** 🚍 **Shuttle bus B**

Borgo Antico (€€)
Piazza di Santo Spirito is a focus for eating, drinking and entertainment, and this is one of its most popular restaurants. It's always busy and bustling, but in summer there are tables outside to escape the thronged interior. Pizzas, set menus and Tuscan staples are all available in generous portions.

✉ **Piazza di Santo Spirito** ☎ **055/210 437** 🚍 **Shuttle bus B**

Cammillo (€€–€€€)
A boisterous, family-run place of long-standing appeal. Don't be fooled by the *faux* rustic interior, for when the bill comes it is likely to be similar to that in other more 'upscale' restaurants. Prices and bustle apart, the food is good, in particular the celebrated *fritto misto*.

✉ **Borgo San Jacopo 57r** ☎ **055/212 427** ⓘ **Closed Tue, Wed & part of Aug** 🚍 **Shuttle bus B**

Casalinga (€)
Sit down with local workers and artisans to tuck in to classic Florentine fare at this cheap and authentic *trattoria*, one of a dying breed in Florence. Located in the street leading east from Piazza di Santo Spirito.

✉ **Via dei Michelozzi 9r** ☎ **055/218 624** ⓘ **Closed Sun & three weeks in Aug** 🚍 **Shuttle bus B**

Quattro Leoni (€–€€)
A welcoming, informal place spread across three airy wood-beamed rooms with modern paintings adorning the medieval stone walls. The food consists of unfussy Florentine standards leavened with the odd twist of culinary invention. Tucked away in a small piazza.

✉ **Via del Vellutini 1r–Piazza della Passera** ☎ **055/218 562** ⓘ **Closed Wed lunch** 🚍 **36, 37 & shuttle bus B & C**

Water
Tuscan and Florentine water in hotels and elsewhere is perfectly safe to drink. Water from drinking fountains in towns is also safe, unless labelled *acqua non potabile*. Bottled water, if you prefer it, is widely available and is invariably ordered with a meal. You may have it fizzy (*acqua gassata* or *con gas*) or still (*acqua naturale*, *liscia* or *non gassata*). Ask for a full bottle (*un litro*), a half bottle (*mezzo litro* or *mezza bottiglia*) or a glass (*un bicchiere*).

Tuscany

Wine and Beer

House wine is *vino della casa*, and in less expensive *trattorie* is sometimes available in half- or quarter litre jugs—ask for *un quarto* or *mezzo litro di vino*. Most beer (*birra*) in Italy is of the yellow, lager-type variety, though darker British-type ale (*birra scura*) is becoming increasingly popular. The least expensive and most usual way to buy beer is from the keg (*una birra alla spina*)—bottled beers, especially foreign ones, are more expensive. The best Italian brands are Peroni, Dreher and Nastro Azzurro. As for size, ask for small (*una birra piccola*)—25cl or 33cl; a *media* (50cl) or a *grande* (litre).

Arezzo

Antica Osteria L'Agania (€)

An authentic and intimate Tuscan *trattoria* (just 40 covers), with a good choice of local dishes based on the region's traditional cooking: things like *polenta, panzanella* (Tuscan salad), *minestrone, ribollita* and *coniglio alla porchetta*. Located just south of Piazza Grande.

✉ **Via Mazzini 10**
☎ **0575/295 381** ⏰ **Closed Mon & part of Jun**

Buca di San Francesco (€–€€)

This is the best-known of Arezzo's restaurants among visitors, largely because it stands close to San Francesco and Piero della Francesca's frescoes. The ambience is a little austere, the food reasonable but not exceptional and the prices a touch over the odds.

✉ **Via San Francesco 1**
☎ **0575/23 271** ⏰ **Closed Mon evening, Tue & Jul**

La Lancia d'Oro (€€)

First choice for a treat, if only for the Piazza Grande setting. Well-executed local specialties such as filling *zuppa di farro* and a variety of tender grilled meats. Fresh fish is sometimes available on Fridays.

✉ **Piazza Grande 18, Logge Vasari** ☎ **0575/21 033**
⏰ **Closed Sun evening & part of Nov**

Il Saraceno (€)

A stone's throw from L'Agania and offering a similarly authentic *trattoria* experience (though with three times as many covers). The food is perhaps a touch better, with superb desserts (try the *marscarpone al caffè*), mouthwatering *ribollita*, succulent *zuppa di porcini* and decadent *ravioli al tartufo*.

✉ **Via Mazzini 6B** ☎ **0575/27 644** ⏰ **Closed Wed & Jul**

Castellina in Chianti

L'Albergaccio (€€)

Any tour of Chianti will probably require a stop for lunch: Castellina has two good options. This is marginally the better and more expensive of the two. The dining room is pretty and in good weather you can eat outdoors. The food is classic Tuscan, with the bonus of homemade pastas.

✉ **Via Fiorentina 63**
☎ **0577/741 042** ⏰ **Closed Sun evening, Thu lunch, Wed & Jan–Feb**

Antica Trattoria La Torre (€€)

This is fine *trattoria* of the old school, with a reliable service. Sundays can be busy, with service slow as a result, so go prepared for a leisurely lunch.

✉ **Piazza del Comune**
☎ **0577/740 236** ⏰ **Closed Fri & two weeks in Sep & Feb**

Colle di Val d'Elsa

L'Antica Trattoria (€€€)

Despite its less than perfect position—in the lower and newer part of Colle on a square bustling with cars and buses—the chances are you will have one of your better Tuscan meals in this superb Michelin-starred restaurant. As well as much-loved staples such as *zuppa di legumi* and *l'anatra all uva* (duck with grapes) patron Enrico Paradisi regularly experiments with new and invariably successful dishes.

 **Piazza Arnolfo 23**
☎ **0577/923 747** ⊕ **Closed Tue, 25 Dec–6 Jan**

Cortona
La Locanda del Loggetta (€€)
Located at the heart of Cortona on a loggia overlooking Piazza della Repubblica, one of the town's main squares. A calm medieval interior, complete with brick vaulting, and assured traditional Italian cooking.
 **Piazza Pescheria 3** ☎ **0575/630 575** ⊕ **Closed Wed & part of Nov**

Il Preludio (€–€€)
Housed in part of a medieval *palazzo* at the heart of Cortona, this pleasant restaurant offers food in a classic Tuscan mould, enlivened with occasional touches of invention. Pastas and *antipasti* are all homemade, the *risotti*, in particular, being especially good.
 **Via Guelfa 11** ☎ **0575/630 104** ⊕ **Closed Mon**

Lucca
La Buca di Sant'Antonio (€€)
Standards are not quite what they were at Lucca's premier restaurant (it has had a Michelin star in the past), but the traditional cooking, central location and pleasant atmosphere still make a winning combination. Dishes perfected over 40 years include *bacalà*, delicate *ravioli di ricotta*, and *risotto*.
 **Via della Cervia 1–3** ☎ **0583/55 881** ⊕ **Closed Sun evening, Mon & parts of Jan & Jul**

Da Leo Fratelli Buralli (€)
A busy, no-frills *trattoria* aimed at providing ravenous Lucchese workers with a reasonably priced lunch. Its central location, however—just off Piazza San Michele—also makes it a good evening option. The cooking has predictable Tuscan-Lucchese leanings.
 **Via Tegrini 1** ☎ **0583/492 236** ⊕ **Closed Sun evening**

Osteria Baralla (€–€€)
Just a few steps from the evocative amphitheatre-shaped Piazza dell'Anfiteato, this simple and popular restaurant is a little off the beaten track and so sees more locals than visitors. It serves unpretentious regional dishes at fair prices.
 **Via dell'Anfiteatro 5** ☎ **0583/440 240** ⊕ **Closed Sun**

Puccini (€€–€€€)
A lovely central restaurant, located a stone's throw from the birthplace of Puccini. Fish and seafood are the menu's sole staples (hence the high prices) with the various *ravioli* a delicious first course choice.
 **Corte San Lorenzo 3** ☎ **0583/316 116** ⊕ **Closed Wed lunch, Tue & Nov–end Feb**

Montalcino

Il Moro (€)
The first choice for a straightforward meal in modern *trattoria* surroundings at prices that will not break the bank.
 **Via Mazzini 44** ☎ **0577/849 384** ⊕ **Closed Thu**

Il Re di Macchia (€€–€€€)
Montalcino has plenty of good restaurants, but this is the smartest. While the food is invariably excellent, it has far more modern (and not always successful) culinary leanings than its more traditional rivals. The wine list is excellent.
 **Via Soccorso Saloni 21** ☎ **0577/846 116** ⊕ **Closed Thu**

After Dinner
The classic after-dinner drink in Tuscany is Vin Santo, or holy wine, an amber dessert wine often drunk with small almond biscuits (*cantucci* or *cantuccini*). The aniseed-flavoured Sambuca and almond-based Amaretto are also well-known, though Italians prefer *amaro* (literally 'bitter'), an almost medicinal tipple of herbs, wines and secret ingredients. The best brands are Averna, Ramazotti and the extremely bitter Fernet-Branca. The best Italian brandy is Vecchia Romagna.

Soft Drinks

Italian bars have a wonderful selection of bottled fruit drinks (*un succo di frutta*) available in varieties such as pear (*pera*), apricot (*albicocca*) and peach (*peach*). Freshly squeezed orange juice is *una spremuta d'arancia*, freshly squeezed grapefruit *una spremuta di pompelmo*. *Lemon Soda* (the brand name) is a popular, refreshing and widely available bitter lemon drink. *Granita* is crushed ice covered in a syrup (usually coffee). A milk shake is *un frullato*, or a *frappé*, if made with ice cream. *Crodini* is a popular but virulently orange non-alcoholic aperitif. Ice is *ghiaccio*; a slice of lemon *uno spicchio di limone*.

Pizzeria San Giorgio (€)

The pizzas here are not the best in the world, but this is the most reasonably priced and easygoing of the town's many good eating places. Pastas and full meals also.

✉ **Via Soccorso Saloni**
☎ **0577/848 507**

Sciame (€–€€)

An informal little bar with a top-rate *trattoria* to one side. Good for well-executed Tuscan basics with a twist.

✉ **Via Ricasoli 9** ☎ **0577/848 017** 🕐 **Closed Tue**

Taverna Grappola Blu (€–€€)

Just two pleasant small stone-walled rooms and often superb and innovative food. Pastas are especially interesting and unusual. Increasingly popular, so be sure to reserve a table. Can be slow at busy times, however, and the piped classical music is unfortunate.

✉ **Via Scale di Moglio 1, signed off Via Mazzini**
☎ **0577/847 150**

Montepulciano

Caffè Poloziano (€–€€)

Montepulciano's nicest café has a lovely art nouveau interior. In addition there is a separate restaurant for full meals.

✉ **Via di Voltaia nel Corso 27–29** ☎ **0578/758 615**
🕐 **Restaurant closed Sun**

Diva (€)

Diva is something of an institution, though it is no longer quite the old-world and undiscovered *trattoria* it once was. The menu is limited—little more than grilled meats for the main course—but all is perfectly

cooked. It's popular and inexpensive, so be sure to arrive early to secure a table. If upstairs is full there is more room downstairs. Located in the lower part of town, just inside the walls.

✉ **Via Gracciano nel Corso 92**
☎ **0578/716 951** 🕐 **Closed Tue & three weeks in Jul**

Il Pozzo (€€)

This restaurant could hardly be in a more perfect gem of a village, and so starts with the advantages of a lovely setting. Its traditional but elevated food is worthy of the location, though some may find dishes such as quail, stuffed pigeon and wild boar in a heavy sauce a little too rich and robust. Simpler food is available at lower prices, though it is usually worth paying extra for the more inventive dishes.

✉ **Piazza Roma 2** ☎ **0577/304 127** 🕐 **Closed Sun evening, Mon, Jan (after Epiphany) & 1 week in Aug**

Pienza

Da Falco (€–€€)

A welcoming, family-run *trattoria* just outside the walls, with several snug dining rooms and plenty of Tuscan specialities. Try the superb *gnocchi* or the *pecorino alla griglia* (sheep's cheese—a Pienzan delicacy—wrapped in ham and grilled).

✉ **Piazza Dante Alighieri 7**
☎ **0578/748 551** 🕐 **Closed Fri**

Latte di Luna (€–€€)

Another friendly and traditional Pienzan restaurant located in an evocative little corner at the eastern end of Pienza's short main street. It is graced with a small terrace

for *al fresco* eating in summer, together with an ancient well incorporated into the medieval interior.

☒ **Via San Carlo 2–4**
☎ **0578/748 606** 🕐 **Closed Tue**

Pisa

Antica Trattoria da Bruno (€€)
This bustling and friendly restaurant is a family affair, where you'll find a good range of Tuscan dishes. Autumn specialities include a number of game dishes and excellent funghi, while good fresh fish is available year-round.

☒ **Via Bianchi 12**
☎ **050/560 818** 🕐 **Closed Mon evening & Tue**

La Mescita (€–€€)
Much loved by locals and students from the nearby university faculties, this central little *trattoria* adds the occasional creative novelty to a menu dominated by a selection of Tuscan staples. Good selection of wines.

☒ **Via Cavalca 2** ☎ **050/544 294** 🕐 **Closed Mon**

Osteria dei Cavalieri (€–€€)
This has traditionally been one of the best-known and better regarded of Pisa's handful of central restaurants. Cooking is not especially distinguished, but the food is mostly reliable, fresh and well prepared. The choice of wines is good, and service generally jovial and accomplished. Located on the street running south from Piazza dei Cavalieri, Pisa's central main square.

☒ **Via San Frediano 16**
☎ **050/580 858** 🕐 **Closed Sat lunch & Sun**

Vineria di Piazza (€)
A simple, inexpensive trattoria, with outside tables, at the heart of the old city. You can sample classic Pisan dishes here, such as *bordatino* (a bean and vegetable soup).

☒ **Piazza delle Vettovaglie 13**
☎ **No phone** 🕐 **Closed Sun & Aug**

Pistoia

San Jacopo (€€)
A thoroughly reliable choice in the historic part of town for venerable Tuscan dishes, including some unique to Pistoia, such as *maccheroni sull'anatra muta* (pasta with duck sauce), traditionally eaten on the feast day of the city's patron saint.

☒ **Via Crispi 15** ☎ **0573/27 786** 🕐 **Closed Tue lunch & Mon**

San Gimignano

Osteria delle Catene (€€)
One of San Gimignano's newer restaurants, but one that has already gained a good reputation. Prices may rise, but the cooking at present makes no down market compromises for the town's large number of tourists.

☒ **Via Mainardi 18**
☎ **0577/941 966** 🕐 **Closed Wed**

Ristorante Dorandò (€€€)
The town's most expensive and most ambitious restaurant prides itself on creating 'historic' dishes of Renaissance and Etruscan vintage. This sounds dubious, but the results are usually excellent. The elegant ambience is offset by deliberately rustic touches.

Seasonal Food

The time of year you visit Tuscany will have a bearing on the food and specialties available. Fruit and vegetables are invariably home grown in Italy, and exotic produce is rarely imported from abroad. January and February see the arrival of oranges from Sicily; asparagus and artichokes appear in early spring; late spring sees cherries in the shops, followed soon after by strawberries, apricots, peaches and plums. Autumn adds grapes and game to the Tuscan menu, notably wild boar (*cinghiale*), as well as seasonal specialities, such as truffles and wild mushrooms, especially the prized *porcini*, eaten grilled or added to pasta or risottos.

Bar Procedure

Tuscan bars may be either smart café-type places or functional refuges for a quick stand-up coffee. In all but the simplest village bars you usually pay a premium to sit down inside or outside, where waiter service is usually the norm. However, a single purchase allows you to sit and watch the world go by almost indefinitely. Standing up, the procedure is to pay for what you want first at the cash desk (*la cassa*) and take your receipt (*lo scontrino*) to the bar to order. In a busy bar a tip slapped down with your receipt often works wonders with the service.

✉ Vicolo dell'Oro 2, off Piazza della Cisterna ☎ 0577/941 862 ⏰ Closed Mon in low season & Jan–end Feb

Ristorante Il Pino (€–€€)

The first choice restaurant (unless you wish to go upscale) in a town with a profusion of restaurants aimed largely at visitors. A pretty interior and plenty of tempting Tuscan tidbits, especially among the mouthwatering *antipasti*.

✉ Via San Matteo 102 ☎ 0577/942 225 ⏰ Closed Thu

Ristorante La Stella (€–€€)

This pleasing but busy restaurant is often crammed with foreigners, thanks mainly to its reputation for good food at reasonable prices. Much of the produce comes from the owners' own farm.

✉ Via San Matteo 75 ☎ 0577/940 444 ⏰ Closed Wed

Le Vecchie Mura (€)

Attractively set in a vaulted former stable, built within the old town walls. The atmosphere is friendly and the meals reasonable, and pizzas are also available in the evening. A good choice for an unpretentious and fairly priced meal.

✉ Via Piandornella 15 ☎ 0577/940 270 ⏰ Closed Tue

Siena
Ai Marsili (€€)

One of Siena's more serious and formal restaurants, and a good place to dress up and treat yourself. Service can be a little brusque, but the food is invariably good and the spacious dining room appealingly medieval.

✉ Via del Castro 3 ☎ 0577/47 154 ⏰ Closed Mon

Antica Osteria da Divo (€€–€€€)

Some remarkable subterranean medieval dining rooms and an upstairs dining area that is almost as evocative: the food is also more than acceptable. Located a little way north of the Duomo.

✉ Via Franciosa 29 ☎ 0577/286 054 ⏰ Closed Sun in winter

Le Campane (€€)

Readers of Siena's local paper, *La Nazione*, voted this their best-loved Sienese restaurant (and their second preference overall across the province of Siena). A nice interior, with a few tables outside in summer, and a very central location.

✉ Via delle Campane 6 ☎ 0577/284 035 ⏰ Closed Mon

Il Campo (€€€)

Most of the restaurants on the Campo are either reasonable but forgettable pizzerias or over-priced tourist traps. However, it's not every day you have the chance to dine out in one of Europe's loveliest squares. So if you want to treat yourself, this is the restaurant to go for. Avoid the four tourist menus and go for the traditional *á la carte* options instead.

✉ Piazza del Campo 50 ☎ 0577/280 725 ⏰ Closed Tue & four weeks in Jan & Feb

Da Enzo (€€)

Currently one of the city's more popular restaurants. The tables are pressed close together, while the walls are

decorated with the symbols of Siena's various *contrade*. The patron prides himself on his ingredients, many of which he produces himself. The daily set menu is good value.

✉ **Via Camollia 49** ☎ **0577/281 277** ⏰ **Closed Sun & a period in Jul**

Garibaldi (€)

An inexpensive and reasonably cheerful *trattoria*, located beneath the small hotel of the same name.

✉ **Via Giovanni Dupré 18** ☎ **0577/284 204** ⏰ **Closed Sat**

Nello (€€)

If Le Logge (almost opposite) is closed or full, or you wish to spend a little less, this easygoing restaurant makes an ideal alternative. You see the day's pasta being made and laid out as you enter—always a good sign—and the food when it arrives lives up to first impressions. A nice single medieval dining room, plus a few tables outside in summer.

✉ **Via del Porrione 28–30** ☎ **0577/289 043** ⏰ **Closed Sun & Jan**

Osteria del Fico Mezzo (€–€€)

A tremendous addition to Siena's rather predictable crop of restaurants: innovative food; a tasteful single-room dining area (cool and pastel-painted); and good value, especially at lunchtime, when you can choose between a handful of set-price mini menus.

✉ **Via dei Termini 71** ☎ **0577/222 384** ⏰ **Closed Sun & mid-Jul to mid-Aug**

Osteria Le Logge (€€)

This is Siena's prettiest restaurant, thanks to its lovely cabinet-lined interior—the building was formerly an old pharmacy. The food, however, once considered outstanding, has slipped recently. Located just a few steps east of the Campo. Be sure to reserve ahead.

✉ **Via del Porrione 33** ☎ **0577/48 013** ⏰ **Closed Sun & Jan**

La Torre (€€)

This rumbustious single room *trattoria*, no longer the undiscovered gem it once was, plays slightly on its old-world authenticity, and prices have risen as a result. However, it remains popular, so arrive early or reserve in person to be sure of a table. Rarely any menu, so follow the advice of the waiter. The off-Campo location is convenient.

✉ **Via Salicotto 7** ☎ **0577/287 548** ⏰ **Closed Thu**

Volterra
Da Badò (€–€€)

An excellent restaurant with a high reputation which is known for its well-cooked Volterran specialties.

✉ **Borgo San Lazzaro 9, just east of Volterra on the SS68 road** ☎ **0588/86 477** ⏰ **Closed Wed & Jul**

Trattoria del Sacco Fiorentino (€–€€)

A newish restaurant which offers classic Tuscan cooking with a slight innovatory twist. Prices in the small adjoining *enoteca* (wine bar) area are lower.

✉ **Piazza XX Settembre 18** ☎ **0588/88 537** ⏰ **Closed Wed & parts of Jan & Feb**

Tea

Tea with lemon (*un tè al limone*) is common in Italy. Tea with milk is not, so you have to ask for it specifically (*tè con latte*) and make sure the milk is cold (*con latte freddo*). Camomile (*camomilla*) is common after dinner in place of coffee, and iced tea (*tè freddo*) is widely available in summer.

Florence

Prices

€   = Up to €100
€€ = €100–€175
€€€ = more than €175

Reservations

Advance booking is always a good idea in Florence and Siena during busy times of the year, though both cities have hotel agencies which will hunt around for last-minute rooms. In Florence the agency (ITA) is on the station concourse of the Santa Maria Novella rail station; in Siena it is called Siena Hotels Promotion and is found on Viale Curatone, near the bus terminal, opposite the church of San Domenico. If you are touring around Tuscany phone a couple of days ahead to secure a room, but note that the idea of credit card advance reservations has not yet really caught on in Italy.

Annalena (€€)

An extremely popular three-star pension-style hotel in the Oltrarno. Housed in an old Medici palace opposite the Boboli gardens. Some of the 20 rooms have terraces and garden views.
✉ **Via Romana 34** ☎ **055/222 402; www.hotelannalena.it**
🚌 **11, 36**

Beacci Tornabuoni (€€€)

A venerable three-star hotel converted from a 14th-century palazzo on Florence's premier shopping street. The 28 rooms are elegantly faded, some smaller and less well furnished than others. There is a pleasant terrace.
✉ **Via dei Tornabuoni 3** ☎ **055/212 645 or 268 377; www.tornabuonihotels.com**
🚌 **6, 11, 36, 37**

Brunelleschi (€€€)

A conversion around a fine medieval tower in a quiet position just behind Via dei Calzaiuoli. An excellent, centrally located four-star hotel, with 96 rooms.
✉ **Piazza Sant'Elisabetta 3** ☎ **055/290 311; www.hotelbrunelleschi.it**
🚌 **In the pedestrian zone: nearest services 1, 6, 7, 11, 14**

Casci (€€)

A delightful family-run two-star hotel about a minute north of Piazza del Duomo. Good rooms.
✉ **Via Cavour 13** ☎ **055/211 686; www.hotelcasci.com**
🚌 **All services to Piazza del Duomo**

Helvetia & Bristol (€€€)

Recent restoration has made this Florence's finest luxury (five-star) hotel. A central position between Via dei Tornabuoni and Piazza della Repubblica makes it an ideal base for shopping and sightseeing.
✉ **Via dei Pescioni 2** ☎ **055/288 353; www.helvetia bristolfirenze.it** 🚌 **6, 11, 36, 37**

Hermitage (€€)

A very well-known three-star hotel overlooking the Ponte Vecchio; very popular with UK and US visitors. Of the 29 rooms, those in the front are double-glazed, those in the back are quieter. Welcoming, family-run atmosphere.
✉ **Vicolo Marzio 1, off Piazza del Pesce** ☎ **055/287 216; www.hermitagehotel.com**
🚌 **Shuttle bus B**

J & J (€€€)

A quiet, small and intimate four-star hotel in a former 16th-century monastery with 19 smart and very tasteful rooms. Located slightly to the east of the main hub. Popular with a select and loyal group of clients, so be certain to reserve well ahead.
✉ **Via di Mezzo 20** ☎ **055/ 263 121; www.jandjhotel.it**
🚌 **Shuttle bus B**

Liana (€–€€)

Housed in an 18th-century palace—the former home of the British Embassy—partly decorated with frescoed ceilings and mosaic floors. Slightly spartan rooms (18), but fine communal parts and a shady garden. Located northeast of central Florence, but within walking distance of Santa Croce and SS. Annunziata. Parking nearby, so a good choice if you are coming by car. Two-star.
✉ **Via V Alfieri 18** ☎ **055/245 303; www.hotelliana.com**
🚌 **Shuttle bus C, 31, 32, 26**

Loggiato dei Serviti (€€–€€€)

An award-winning conversion in the vaulted interior of the Servites' former 16th-century confraternity building. Subtle, calm and airy rooms (29); advance reservations essential. An excellent mid-priced choice (three-star).

✉ **Piazza Santissima Annunziata 3** ☎ **055/289 592; fax 055/289 595** 🚌 **6, 31, 32**

Lungarno (€€–€€€)

A reasonably modern four-star Oltrarno hotel whose comfortable rooms (68) are divided between a new block (some with views of the river and Ponte Vecchio) and a converted 13th-century tower. The best rooms have terraces and views; all are decorated with antiques and a selection of the hotel's large collection of modern art.

✉ **Borgo San Jacopo 14** ☎ **055/27 261;** **www.lungarnohotels.com** 🚌 **Shuttle bus B or C**

Morandi alla Crocetta (€€–€€€)

A small and welcoming three-star hotel that forms part of a peaceful former 16th-century monastery just east of Piazza Santissima Annunziata. Ten rooms.

✉ **Via Laura 50** ☎ **055/234 4747; www.hotelmorandi.it** 🚌 **1, 6, 7, 10, 11, 17**

Porta Faenza (€€)

One of the better hotels close to the station and San Lorenzo market area. Spacious rooms with modern fittings. Three-star.

✉ **Via Faenza 77** ☎ **055/284 119; www.hotelportafaenza.it** 🚌 **All services to Santa Maria Novella rail station**

Porta Rossa (€€)

Housed in a 14th-century palace: one of the oldest hotels in Italy. Byron and Stendhal both stayed here. Three-star, 78 rooms.

✉ **Via Porta Rosa 19** ☎ **055/287 551;** **www.hotelportarossa.com** 🚌 **In the pedestrian zone: nearest services 6,11,31,32,36,37**

Residenza (€€)

Good value, given the excellent location, though rooms on the street can be noisy. Acceptable if rather unexciting rooms (24) ranged across the top floors of a 17th-century *palazzo*. Three-star.

✉ **Via dei Tornabuoni 8** ☎ **055/218 684;** **www.laresidenzahotel.com** 🚌 **6, 11, 36, 37**

Scaletta (€–€€)

Located on the top floor of a 15th-century palace and usually remarkably peaceful given the Oltrarno location. Spacious and simply furnished rooms (13), together with two excellent terraces with views looking towards the Palazzo Pitti and Giardino di Boboli.

✉ **Via Guicciardini 13** ☎ **055/283 028 ;** **www.hotellascaletta.it** 🚌 **11, 37 & shuttle buses B & C**

Sorelle Bandini (€)

Spacious rooms (13) of crumbling grandeur in a 16th-century palace of considerable Bohemian charm. Excellent value and often reserved months ahead as a result. One-star.

✉ **Piazza Santo Spirito 9** ☎ **055/215 308; fax 055/282 761** 🚌 **36, 37 & shuttle bus B**

Westin Excelsior (€€€€)

On balance the better of the two famous and grand old hotels on this rather lacklustre square by the river. The 160 rooms are nicely old-world in look and feel, and most have more character than those of the *Grand* opposite.

✉ **Piazza Ognissanti 3** ☎ **055/264 201; www.westin.com** 🚌 **11, 17 & shuttle bus C**

Location

Where you stay in Florence is not of prime importances since most of the central sights are within easy walking distance of the major hotels. Less expensive hotels tend to be close to the station, which is less salubrious than elsewhere, without being too unpleasant. Also note the problems of noise (see panel ➤ 105) and be sure you are not in a peripheral hotel if taking a package or reservation through an agency. In Tuscany many tour companies reserve hotels in Chianciano, an unlovely spa town with little to recommend it unless you are taking the waters. Even with a car it is inconvenient for most of the region's best sights.

Tuscany

Costs and Ratings

Italian hotels are rated from one-star (basic) to five-star (luxury), with the price for each room within a hotel being fixed by law (it should be clearly displayed on the room door or close by). However, prices for rooms can vary within a hotel, so if you are not happy with your room ask to see another. Hotels in lower categories may also have less expensive rooms without private bathrooms. Look out for hidden extras, notably breakfast, which may be included in the room rate (check the back of the door, where the information should be displayed with the room price). Usually it is extra and exorbitant, making it better to take breakfast in a bar if you have the choice. Supplements may also be levied for air-conditioning.

Arezzo

Cavaliere Palace (€€)

Located in a quiet side street and a touch smarter than its nearby rival. The four-star hotel was recently updated, so the modern rooms (27) are bright and new.

✉ **Via Madonna del Prato 83**
☎ **0575/268 36;**
www.cavalierehotels.com

Cortona

Hotel San Luca (€€)

A modern four-star hotel; many of the 56 rooms enjoy fine views of the valley.

✉ **Piazza Garibaldi 1–2**
☎ **0575/630 460;**
www.sanlucacortona.co,

Hotel San Michele (€€)

A glorious Renaissance *palazzo* whose elegance was retained following its conversion into a four-star, 55-room hotel. Plenty of old-world grandeur, and some antique-filled period rooms. Central location.

✉ **Via Guelfa 15** ☎ **0575/604 348; www.hotelsanmichele.net**

Lucca

Hotel Universo (€€)

Lucca's best-known traditional hotel. Many of the 60 comfortable old rooms retaining an air of faded grandeur: some have views over the piazza. Three-star.

✉ **Piazza del Giglio 1**
☎ **0583/493 678;**
www.universolucca.com

La Luna (€–€€)

Centrally located close to the evocative Piazza Anfiteatro. The 30 rooms are a mixture of old and new, some with wooden ceilings. Three-star.

✉ **Corte Compagni 12, off Via Fillungo** ☎ **0583/493 634; www.hotellaluna.com**

Piccolo Hotel Puccini (€–€€)

A splendid central position close to Piazza San Michele. Pleasant and well-presented rooms (14), though the communal parts are a little cramped. Three-star.

✉ **Via di Poggio 9** ☎ **0583/55 421; fax 0583/53 487**

Montalcino

Dei Capitani (€€–€€€)

An excellent central three-star hotel which opened in 1996. Rooms (29) to the rear, plus the bar and terrace have lovely views. Small panoramic swimming pool.

✉ **Via Lapini 6, below Piazza Cavour** ☎ **0577/847 227; www.deicapitani.it**

Il Giglio (€–€€)

An inn for over a century, this moderately elegant three-star hotel in central Montalcino has recently been improved by renovation work. Many of the 12 rooms enjoy views over the *crete* and Orcia valley.

✉ **Via Soccorso Saloni 5**
☎ **0577/848 167;**
www.gigliohotel.com

Montepulciano

Duomo (€–€€)

This is the best all-round mid-priced hotel in town. Located a few metres (yards) up the street from the cathedral square. Be sure to reserve ahead.

✉ **Via San Donato 14**
☎ **0578/757 473;**
www.albergoduomolibero.it

Pienza

Il Chiostro di Pienza Relais (€€–€€€)

This new and beautifully converted three-star hotel is centrally located; the 37 tasteful rooms form part of a former monastery and are entered from an elegant courtyard (*chiostro*).

✉ **Corso Il Rossellino 26**
☎ **0578/748 400; www.relaisilchiostrodipienza.com**

Corsignano (€€)
A modern and comfortable three-star hotel with slightly twee rooms (40), about 150m (164yds) west of Piazza Dante and the town walls.
✉ **Via della Madonnina 11**
☎ **0578/748 501; fax 0578/748 166**

Pisa
Touring (€€)
One of the best of a crop of impersonal hotels around the station. The 34 rooms are not terribly large, but all are modern if slightly functional.
✉ **Via Puccini 24 (off the northeast flank of Piazza della Stazione)** ☎ **050/46 374; www.hoteltouringpisa.com**

Pistoia
Leon Bianco (€€)
A central and reasonably peaceful position just south of Piazza del Duomo. Rooms on Via Cavour are perhaps less preferable than those away from the street. Three-star, 27 rooms.
✉ **Via Panciatichi 2**
☎ **0573/26 675;**
www.hotelleonbianco.it

San Gimignano
La Cisterna (€€)
There is little to choose between San Gimignano's major central hotels: La Cisterna has 49 pleasing rooms and a perfect position at the heart of everything. Try for rooms with country or piazza views. Three-star.
✉ **Piazza della Cisterna 24**
☎ **0577/940 328; fax 0577/942 080**

Leon Bianco (€€)
An elegant three-star hotel in a medieval town house, more intimate than La Cisterna with 24 rooms.

✉ **Piazza della Cisterna 13**
☎ **0577/941 294;**
www.leonbianco.com

Siena
Antica Torre (v€)
Eight tasteful, mid-sized rooms in a converted medieval tower make this the most intimate and stylish mid-price option in the city. Reserve ahead.
✉ **Via Fiera Vecchia 7**
☎ **0577/222 255;**
www.anticatorresiena.it

Duomo (€€)
The 23 rooms are unexciting, though perfectly adequate and a good location Three-star.
✉ **Via Stalloreggi 38**
☎ **0577/289 088;**
www.hotelduomo.it

Palazzo Ravizza (€€–€€€)
A peaceful three-star hotel in a peripheral but charming part of the city. A pension since 1929, and recently extensively restored, it is housed in an 18th-century *palazzo*; 30 rooms of varying quality and charm. Reservations essential.
✉ **Pian dei Mantellini 34**
☎ **0577/280 462;**
www.palazzoravizza.it

Piccolo Hotel Etruria (€)
The nicest and thus most popular two-star hotel in the city, so the 13 rooms are quickly snapped up. Reserve in advance.
✉ **Via delle Donzelle 3**
☎ **0577/288 088;**
www.hoteletruria.com

Tre Donzelle (€)
A good, central, budget option but very well-known so reserve in advance. One-star.
✉ **Via delle Donzelle 5**
☎ **0577/280 358; fax 0577/223 933**

Volterra
Etruria (€–€€)
A reasonably priced three-star hotel on the main street in central Volterra.
✉ **Via Matteotti 32** ☎ **0588/87 377; www.albergoetruria.it**

Noise
Noise of all descriptions is a fact of Italian life, whether you are in the countryside—bells and barking dogs—or the city (Vespas, cars, sirens, domestic discord, early-morning street cleaners, church bells and late-night party-goers). Not even the most expensive hotels in Florence are immune to noise, though those with air-conditioning suffer fewer problems (hot summer nights mean you often have to have windows open). If you are a light sleeper, watch out for rooms on the street or busy piazza, and where possible ask for a back, garden or courtyard room. Better still, go armed with earplugs.

Florence

Tempting Toiletries

One of the world's oldest pharmacies, Officina di Santa Maria Novella has been in business since 1612 and still boasts frescoes, antique furniture and old-fashioned fittings. Many products are still made to recipes devised centuries ago by Dominican monks, and all rely only on natural ingredients and traditional production procedures. The soaps and creams are especially good and the potpourri is irresistible. This beautiful shop is located on Via della Scala 16 (☎ 055/216 276, 230 2437 or 288 658).

Books, Maps and Guides

Feltrinelli

An excellent central book shop with plenty of foreign titles, maps and guides.
✉ Via Cavour 12–20r
☎ 055/219 524 🚍 6, 17, 23

Libreria Le Monnier

For years this has been one of the most professional book shops in the city. Italian and international titles. Cultured and helpful staff.
✉ Via San Gallo 53r, one block west of Via Cavour ☎ 055/483 215 or 496 095 🚍 1, 6, 7

Fashion

Pucci (see below) is just one of many leading designer stores in the streets and squares on and around Via dei Tornabuoni and the nearby Via della Vigna Nuova. These include:

Armarni
✉ Via della Vigna Nuova 51r
☎ 055/219 041

Emporio Armarni
✉ Piazza Strozzi 14–17r
☎ 055/284 315

Enrico Coveri
✉ Via della Vigna Nuova 27
☎ 055/281 003

Gucci
✉ Via dei Tornabuoni 73r
☎ 055/264 011

Prada
✉ Via dei Tornabuoni 51r–53r
☎ 055/283 439

Emilio Pucci

The *doyen* of Florentine designers, Pucci has been creating beautiful clothes since the heady *dolce vita* days of the 1950s. The *haute couture* collection is shown in the Palazzo dei Pucci, the ready-to-wear range in the shops listed below.
✉ Via dei Tornabuoni 20–22r
☎ 055/294 028 🚍 In the pedestrian zone
✉ Palazzo Pucci, Via de' Pucci 6 ☎ 055/283 061 🚍 1, 6, 7, 11, 17, 23

Marcella

Florentine women in the know come here for the sleekest lingerie as well as a selection of the timeless clothes and accessories that have seen the shop prosper since its birth as a tiny boutique 30 years ago. An equally enticing men's shop has also opened.
Woman's Shop ✉ Via dei Pecori 8r ☎ 055/213 162
🚍 In the pedestrian zone
Man's Shop ✉ Marcella Uomo, Via Cerretani 7r ☎ 055/216 352 🚍 In the pedestrian zone

Max Mara

One of Italy's leading mid-range designer labels, with classic, simply cut clothes at affordable prices, aimed at a slightly younger market.
✉ Via dei Pecori 23r
☎ 055/287 761 🚍 In the pedestrian zone
✉ Max & Co, Via dei Calzaiuoli 89r ☎ 055/294 292
🚍 In the pedestrian zone

Valentino

One of the great names of Italian fashion, whose clothes have been selling to the rich and famous for nearly 40 years.
✉ Via dei Tosinghi 52r
☎ 055/293 142 🚍 In the pedestrian zone

Food and Wine

Cantinone del Gallo Nero
The Gallo Nero (Black

Cockerel) is one of the most respected consortiums of loosely affiliated Chianti producers. This pretty cellar wine bar sells samples of their products.

✉ Via Santo Spirito 6r ☎ 055/218 898 🚌 Shuttle bus B

Pegna

Pegna has been in the business of selling mouth-watering food since 1860. The supermarket layout is a boon for those whose Italian may not be up to ordering in small delicatessens.

✉ Via dello Studio 8r
☎ 055/282 701 🚌 In the pedestrian zone

Household Goods

Bartolini

Bartolini was founded in 1921 and has become a fixture of Florentine life. It sells a range of kitchen and homeware, including leading Italian and international brands of glassware, china and porcelain.

✉ Via dei Servi 30r
☎ 055/289 223 🚌 6, 31, 32

Mazzoni

Florentines have been coming to Mazzoni to buy linens, towels and fabrics for over a century.

✉ Via Orsanmichele 14r
☎ 055/215 153 🚌 In the pedestrian zone

La Ménagère

A family-owned store founded in 1901 with several floors devoted to glassware, china, furniture and other items for the home.

✉ Via dei Ginori 8r
☎ 055/213 875 🚌 In the pedestrian zone

Jewellery

Caputi

One of the most famous names in top-class Italian

costume jewellery. Also at Borgo Santi Apostoli 44–46r.

✉ Via Santo Spirito 58r
☎ 055/212 972 🚌 Shuttle bus B or C

Lapini

This historic store sells high-quality stones, settings and watches in a variety of traditional and modern designs.

✉ Via dei Cimatori 34r
☎ 055/277 6452 🚌 In the pedestrian zone

Parenti

Florentines in search of the perfect gift often make a beeline for this lovely and legendary shop. Silverware, porcelain, glass, ceramics, candles and jewellery.

✉ Via dei Tornabuoni 93r
☎ 055/214 438 🚌 6, 11

Torrini

Jacopo Torrini patented his mark in 1369. Six centuries later one of his descendants still runs one of the city's most distinguished jewellers.

✉ Piazza del Duomo 10r
☎ 055/230 2401 🚌 In the pedestrian zone

Vincenti

One of all the many old shops on the Ponte Vecchio, this jewellery shop has been here since the 16th century.

✉ Ponte Vecchio 16r
☎ 055/287 241 or 291 065
🚌 In the pedestrian zone

Leather Goods

Cellerini

Most Florentines wanting a bag make straight for this famous store. Some 600 different types of handbag and other luggage hang from the Renaissance ceiling of the 16th-century *palazzo* in which the shop is housed.

✉ Via del Sole 37r, off Via della Spada ☎ 055/282 533
🚌 6, 11 & shuttle bus C to Via dei Tornabuoni

Mercato Centrale

Florence's vast central market is an essential port of call, whether or not you intend to buy anything. Bursting with life, its countless stalls sell a wide variety of fish, fruit, meat, bread and vegetables, together with all manner of delicacies such as hams, truffles, wild boar, cheese, honey, herbs, olive oil and plump porcini mushrooms. The market building, constructed in 1874, is one of Europe's oldest covered food halls and was artfully extended in 1980 without destroying its wonderfully flamboyant atmosphere. Located at Piazza del Mercato Centrale; market days Mon–Fri 7–2, Sat 7–2, 4–8.

Supermarkets

The most prestigious department store in Florence is COIN, conveniently situated at the pedestrianized heart of the city in Via dei Calzaiuoli (☎ 055/280 531; www.coin.it). It sells own-label and designer clothes, linens, kitchenware and a wide variety of general goods. Rinascente is similar, and also forms part of a chain found all over Italy. It sells reasonably priced clothes and other goods from a large central store at Piazza della Repubblica 1 (☎ 055/239 8544; www.rinascente.it).

Montalcino Wine Shops

Numerous shops around Montalcino sell the peerless Brunello di Montalcino, Tuscany's finest red wine, and the less-exalted but high quality Rosso di Montalcino. The following are the most pleasant or offer the best selections.

✉ Co-op, Via Ricasoli, near Sant'Agostino. The Co-op supermarket has a surprisingly good selection of local wines at very competitive prices.

✉ Fiaschetteria Italiana, Pizza del Popolo. A lovely 19th-century café with a smart little *enoteca* to the rear.

✉ Fortezza, Pizzale-Fortezza. Montalcino's castle contains a busy and well-stocked wine shop.

✉ Enoteca Luciani-Grotta del Brunello, Via S Saloni. Has one of the town's bigger selections of wines, grappas and olive oil.

Madova

This celebrated shop was founded in 1919 and sells a variety of beautiful gloves.

✉ **Via Guicciardini 1r**
☎ **055/239 6526** 🚌 **Shuttle buses B & C**

Raspini

This designer name is a byword among Florentines for high-quality shoes, belts and other leather and fashion goods. There are several branches, including Via Roma 25r and Via Martinelli 1–5r.

✉ **Via Por Santa Maria 72r**
☎ **055/215 796** 🚌 **In the pedestrian zone north of the Ponte Vecchio**

Paper and Stationery

Il Papiro

Papiro is a chain of stationers selling marbled paper and marbled paper goods at keener prices than the city's more famous names.

✉ **Via dei Tavolini 13r, off Via dei Calzaiuoli** ☎ **055/213 823**
🚌 **In the pedestrian zone**
✉ **Via Cavour 55r** ☎ **055/215 262** 🚌 **1, 6, 7**

Parione

This shop has been open a mere 80 years, so it is not quite as famous or venerable as Pineider (see below). However, it is still a superb source of paper, pens, visiting cards, marbled paper and leather-bound books.

✉ **Via del Parione 10r, off Piazza Santa Trinita** ☎ **055/215 684** 🚌 **6 or 11 to Piazza Santa Trinita-Via dei Tornabuoni**

Pineider

This celebrated stationery shop has been in Piazza della Signoria since 1774. Napoleon, Byron, Shelley, Puccini, Stendhal and Maria Callas are just a few of the famous who have corresponded on this paper.

Elizabeth Taylor ordered visiting cards from the company to match her eyes.

✉ **Piazza della Signoria 13r**
☎ **055/284 655** 🚌 **In the pedestrian zone**

Il Torchio

First-rate traditional Florentine marbled paper available either in sheets or as part of small paper-covered goods.

✉ **Via dei Bardi 17** ☎ **055/234 2862** 🚌 **Shuttle buse B & C**

Prints

Giovanni Baccani

There are shops selling prints, engravings and paintings in every corner of the city, but the selection at this charming and pretty shop, established in 1903, is so good that you won't need to go anywhere else. Prices range from very reasonable to very prohibitive to suit all budgets.

✉ **Via della Vigna Nuova 75r**
☎ **055/214 467** 🚌 **6, 11, 31, 32**

Shoes

Beltrami

A well-known nationwide chain which sells not only shoes but a small selection of jackets.

✉ **Via della Vigna Nuova 70r**
☎ **055/287 779** 🚌 **6, 11 & shuttle bus C**

Fratelli Rossetti

Another country-wide chain for expensive high-quality shoes.

✉ **Piazza della Repubblica 43–5r** ☎ **055/216 656** 🚌 **In the pedestrian zone**

Salvatore Ferragamo

This famous name has its origins planted in Florence. The city's flagship store contains a fascinating museum dedicated to the exquisite shoes made by the company over the years.

✉ **Via dei Tornabuoni 14r**
☎ **055/292 123** 🚌 **6, 11**

Tuscany

Tuscany's smaller towns and villages—Siena excepted—are not great shopping places. This said, many areas are known for a particular craft or food specialties.

Arts and Crafts

Most Tuscan towns have at least one shop selling ceramics and terracotta. The best choice, however, is found in more touristy towns such as Siena (▶ 86–91) and San Gimignano, though prices here are over rather the odds. With terracotta look for factories on the outskirts of towns which sell directly to the public. Volterra is crammed with shops selling alabaster products, while Lucca, Pisa and the towns of the Versilia coast (Massa and Carrara) have many outlets selling the marble for which the region is famous. Linens and textiles are another good buy, with Lucca in particular having been renowned for centuries for its silk.

Food and Markets

Olive oil, one of Tuscany's most famous exports, need not be bought in fancy bottles at elevated prices. Perfectly good oils can be purchased from the region's many excellent Co-op supermarkets. Pienza's sheep's cheese (*pecorino*) is highly regarded, as is the honey of Montalcino and Siena's spicy *panforte*. Every town has good food shops; most have a weekly market. The following are the best.

Lucca

This market in Via dei Bacchettoni, on the town's eastern fringes, is a general market of clothes, flowers and household goods. The Piazza del Carmine market is a covered food market.

✉ **Piazza del Bacchettoni**
🕒 **Daily**
✉ **Piazza del Carmine**
🕒 **Wed & Sat am**

Montalcino

Old-fashioned market full of locals in the shadow of the town's fairy-tale fortress.

✉ **Piazzale Fortezza** 🕒 **Fri 7–1**

Montepulciano

A big bustling market by the old walls in the lower town.

✉ **Porta al Prato** 🕒 **Thu am**

Pienza

A tiny but interesting market just outside the old walls of the village.

✉ **Viale Mencatelli**
🕒 **Fri am**

Pistoia

✉ **Piazza della Sala**
🕒 **Wed & Sat am**

San Gimignano

An intimate little market in the village's main square.

✉ **Piazza del Duomo**
🕒 **Thu & Sat 7–1**

Siena

The general market in La Lizza is a huge affair. Piazza del Mercato is where many Sienese shop for everyday fruit and vegetables.

✉ **La Lizza, Viale Cesare Maccari** 🕒 **Wed am**
✉ **Piazza del Mercato**
🕒 **Mon–Sat 7–1**

Volterra

A little market in one of the town's central main squares.

✉ **Piazza dei Priori** 🕒 **Sat 7.30–1.30**

Food Heaven

One of Tuscany's finest delicatessens, Maganelli, is found at the heart of Siena (Via di Città 73), its old-fashioned interior crammed with countless wines and brandies, 150 different grappas, 20 different balsamic vinegars, and shelf upon shelf of bottled jams, honeys, tomatoes, mushrooms, *pesto*, onions and other mouthwatering Tuscan specialties. It also has a good selection of Sienese delicacies such as *panforte* and *cantuccini*, the latter a special almond biscuit for dipping in dessert wines such as Vin Santo.

Florence

Italy and Children
Florence in summer can be a tough place for children, who can be forgiven for growing fractious in the heat and bored with the endless round of museums and historic buildings. At the same time, the Italians have a far more open-minded attitude to children than many (the smaller and blonder the better) and will usually make special provisions for them in hotels and restaurants. Children can ease the way in dealings with waiters, hotel staff and Italian officialdom in all its guises.

Food
Italian treats can save many a situation. Few children should be able to resist ice cream, while a pizza by the slice (*pizza taglia*) from bakeries can also work wonders. Fresh-made milk shakes (*frullati* or *frappé*) may also win children over, as may roast chestnuts from a streetside vendor in autumn or winter. The novelty of breakfast in a bar, or at an outside table, may also appeal.

Ice cream

Bondi (€)
This outlet near the station has some of the most exotic concoctions in the city.
☒ **Via Nazionale 61r**
☎ **055/287 490**

Carabé (€)
Come here for a *granita* (crushed ice with a choice of fruit syrup) or a tub of the excellent pistachio ice cream.
☒ **Via Ricasoli 60r**
☎ **055/289 476**

Festival del Gelato (€)
Children will have trouble choosing from over 100 varieties on offer.
☒ **Via del Corso 75r**
☎ **055/294 386**

Perché No! (€)
A central *gelateria* which has been in business since 1939.
☒ **Via dei Tavolini 19r**
☎ **055/239 8969**

Vivoli (€)
Vivoli is home to the very best ice cream in Florence—perhaps even in Italy.
☒ **Via Isole delle Stinche 7r**
☎ **055/292 334**

Galleries and Museums
There is no reason why children should not enjoy a small dose of carefully chosen culture. Michelangelo's *David* is a good place to start (► 19). The detailed narrative of Gozzoli's frescoes in the Palazzo Medici-Riccardi may captivate, as may the comprehensible frescoes of Fra Angelico in San Marco (► 23). The armour and Giambologna's menagerie in the Bargello should also be popular (► 22). Diverting museums include the Museo di Storia della Scienza (► 45), Museo dei Ragazzi (in the Palazzo Vecchio ► 50) and Museo della Antica Casa Fiorentina (► 39).

Sights
The tremendous view from the Campanile should appeal to children (► 33), though you may well have trouble coaxing them up all the stairs (note that children may not enjoy the slightly claustrophobic passages of the cathedral dome). The Forte di Belvedere (see walk ► 41) is also attractive for similarly panoramic reasons and has the added bonus that children can clamber around the walls and battlements and let off steam. Children may also enjoy the sights and sounds, never mind the potential presents, of the Mercato Centrale and San Lorenzo street market. Be sure to hunt out the famous 'Porcellino', a much-loved bronze boar. The obvious novelty of the Ponte Vecchio should also appeal.

Tuscany

Outdoors

The Giardino di Boboli (➤ 38) is the most obvious place to let children off the leash in Florence. Further afield the chances for kids to run wild are more abundant. The novelty of lanscapes such as the *crete* south of Siena (➤ 92) may appeal more to older children, while the open spaces, wildlife and roam-at-will possibilties of the Alpi Apuane and Monte Amiata are also a possibility (➤ 12–13).

Beaches

The easiest beaches to reach from Florence are those of Viareggio, an elegant seaside resort about an hour from Florence on the train (regular seaside 'specials' run from the city in the summer). The sand is clean and the water safe, though many of the beaches are private—you pay a small fee to enjoy access to the sand, showers, bar and changing rooms. Further south, the (free) beach at Marina di Alberese (21km/13 miles from Grosseto) is among the best in Tuscany but is only accessible by car.

Sights

The towers and streets of San Gimignano (➤ 80) should conjure up evocative medieval images for most children, as should the Campo and Torre della Mangia in Siena (➤ 85). Views from the tops of the towers in these towns and in Lucca (➤ 70) should also appeal, along with the old walls and fortresses of Montalcino (➤ 74), Monteriggioni (➤ 83) and Pienza (➤ 76). The Leaning Tower of Pisa, probably familier to many children from pictures, will probably be as astonishing in real life for kids as it is for adults.

Galleries and Museums

As in Florence, older children should find many of Tuscany's museums and art galleries appealing in small doses. One of Tuscany's most popular Sunday excursions is to the Museo Leonardiano, a museum in the village of Vinci devoted to Leonardo da Vinci.

Museo Leonardiano

This interesting museum features beautiful models of Leonardo da Vinci's inventions drawn up from his notebooks, plus fascinating displays on the artist as inventor and engineer.
🖂 **Castello dei Conti Guidi, Vinci (11km/7 miles north of Empoli)** ☎ **0571/56 055**
🕙 **Daily 9.30–7 (6pm in winter)**
💵 **Moderate**

Parco di Pinocchio

One of the few sights specifically aimed at children is the Parco di Pinocchio. The storybook character was created by Carlo Lorenzini (1826–90), who took his pen name from the village of Collodi where his mother was born. Located 15km (9 miles) east of Lucca, the park has pretty walkways through woods. There are mosaics depicting episodes from Pinocchio's 'life', various monsters, sharks and tableaux, and a toy shop.
🖂 **Parco di Pinocchio, Collodi** ☎ **0572/429 342 or 429 613; www.pinocchio.it** 🕙 **Daily 8.30–dusk** 💵 **Moderate**

Child Reductions

Children qualify for reductions on admittance charges in most Tuscan and Florentine museums and art galleries, though the idea of reduced price 'family' tickets has yet to catch on. Half-price tickets are also available for children under 12 on most buses and trains. Children under four travel free on trains. There are also reductions for families, worth considering if you intend to travel widely by train. Inquire about the Rail Europe Family Card (known as the *Carta Rail Europe F* in Italy) or Italy's own *Carta Famiglia* (available from main stations). The latter allows families of four visiting together to claim discounts of 30 per cent on the full fare. Few restaurants cater specifically for children by offering half-priced half portions, though most will provide reduced portions at reduced prices if you ask.

Florence

Obtaining Tickets

Tickets for most events can usually be obtained from the box office of the venue concerned. However, it can often be easier to use one of several commercial ticket agencies dotted around the city. The most central is Box Office, which has outlets at Via Almanni 39 (☎ 055/210 804) and Chiasso dei Soldanieri 8r, off Via Porta Rossa at the corner with Via dei Tornabuoni (☎ 055/219 402).

Information

Listings of current and forthcoming events can be obtained from the tourist office (which has lots of posters and pamphlets); from the pages of newspapers such as *La Nazione* and *La Repubblica*; and from listings magazines such as *Metro*, *Firenze Spettacolo*, *Time Off* and the English-language *Events*.

Classical Music

Florence's main classical music events take place during its big summer festivals (see below). During the rest of the year numerous smaller recitals of music are held in the city's churches and concert halls.

Amici della Musica

A group known as the Amici della Musica organizes an October to April season of Saturday afternoon concerts (usually at the Teatro della Pergola or the Teatro Goldini).
⊠ **Box office: Via Alammani 39** ☎ **055/210 084. Information: 055/607 440**
Teatro della Pergola ⊠ **Via della Pergola 18** ☎ **055/247 9651; Teatro Goldini** ⊠ **Via Santa Maria 15** ☎ **055/210 804**

Musicus Concertus

Another association, the Musicus Concertus, holds recitals between October and June at various city locations, including the auditorium of the Palazzo dei Congressi.
⊠ **Piazza del Carmine 19** ☎ **055/287 347**

Orchestera Regionale

Another name to look for is the Orchestra Regionale Toscana, which often presents chamber concerts in churches such as Santo Stefano.
⊠ **Via delle Pesce, (off Via Por Santa Maria) or Teatro Verdi** ☎ **055/234 0710**

Palazzo dei Congressi
⊠ **Viale F Strozzi (north of the rail station)** ☎ **No phone**

Teatro Comunale

The Teatro Comunale, the city's key performance venue, runs its own season of smaller concerts from September to mid-December, together with opera performances (Dec–end Jan) and occasional symphony concerts (Jan–end Apr).
⊠ **Corso Italia 16, off Lungarno Amerigo Vespucci** ☎ **055/277 9236** 🚌 **Shuttle bus C**

Teatro Verdi

The slightly smaller Teatro Verdi mixes opera and ballet productions with its theatrical repertoire between January and April.
⊠ **Via Ghibellina 101** ☎ **055/212 320** 🚌 **14**

Clubs, Discos and Live Music

Andromeda

A popular and very central club-disco that regularly changes its interior appearance to keep up with latest trends.
⊠ **Via dei Cimatori 13-Vicolo dei Cerchi** ☎ **055/292 002** 🕐 **Closed Sun** 🚌 **In the pedestrian zone**

Auditorium Flog

Currently the city's best-known and most important venue for live rock and jazz

concerts. Hosts occasional one-off 'specials' devoted to particular musical genres. See listings for details.
✉ **Via Mercanti 24b** ☎ **055/487 145** 🚌 **4**

Full Up
Many Florentine clubs and discos rise and fall quite quickly: This place has been around for some time and is especially popular with a slightly older, more refined crowd at the weekends.
✉ **Via della Vigna Vecchia 21, off Via del Proconsolo**
☎ **055/293 006** 🚌 **19**

Jazz Club
A club that plays jazz, as its name suggests, with serious music and appreciative audiences. You need to obtain membership to enter, but this is easily done at the door.
✉ **Via Nuova dei Caccini 3** ☎ **055/247 9700** 🚌 **6, 12, 14, 23, 71**

Maracanà
A lively Latin American disco housed in a former theatre, near to the railway station. You can eat a pizza looking down on the circular dance floor from the restaurant balcony. Maracanà also presents an occasional, but very entertaining, Brazilian cabaret and floor show.
✉ **Via Faenza 4** ☎ **055/210 298** 🚌 **All services to the rail station**

Meccanò
This is probably the most popular disco in the city, although not the most central. Meccanò is situated some way to the west of central Florence, by the Cascine park.
✉ **Piazza Vittorio Veneto**
☎ **055/331 371** 🕐 **Closed Mon** 🚌 **17c**

Rex
Young or old, you'll find Rex one of the most welcoming and easygoing of Florence's late-night bar-clubs. Don't be put off by the striking decor. There's plenty of room for a drink (cocktails are good) or light snack, and at weekends DJs provide the musical backdrop.
✉ **Via Fiesolana 25r**
☎ **055/248 0331** 🚌 **Shuttle bus B**

Space Electronic
Equally popular with Florentines and visitors, this packed club pulls in the crowds with its eminently danceable range of mainstream rock and pop, with 1970s numbers for the young-at-heart.
✉ **Via Palazzuolo 37**
☎ **055/293 082/293 457**

Tenax
Tenax is the city's largest disco and is popular with visitors and Florentines alike. However, its peripheral position—out in the direction of the airport—means it is much more likely to appeal to dedicated clubbers only. Do give some advance thought as to how you will get home.
✉ **Via Pratese 46a, Peretola**
☎ **055/308 160** 🚌 **Best to take a taxi**

Yab
Florence's larger clubs and discos tend to be on the city's fringes: Yab is central, and as a result tends to attract both visitors and a local crowd, which, with the familiar dance music, makes for an enjoyable evening.
✉ **Via dei Sassetti 5r**
☎ **055/290 608 or 055/210 884**
🚌 **In the pedestrian zone**

Cinemas
Virtually all new and old movies shown in Italy are dubbed into Italian, and Florence has a very limited selection of cinemas that offer films in their original language (*versione originale*). If you want to catch a movie during your stay, try the Cinema Goldoni in the Oltrarno (✉ Via dei Serragli 109 ☎ 055/222 437 🕐 Closed Jun–Jul), which usually shows movies in English three times weekly.

Dance

National and international dance troupes tend to save their best for Florence's two big summer festivals, the Maggio Musicale Fiorentino and Estate Fiesolana (see main text). However, both the Teatro Comunale and Teatro della Pergola offer ballet performances as part of their regular seasons. Consult the tourist office for details of forthcoming events.

Music Festivals

Maggio Musicale Fiorentino

Florence's premier cultural event is the Maggio Musicale Fiorentino, an internationally renowned festival of opera and classical music held between late April and early July. The festival has its own orchestra, chorus and ballet troupe, but alternates its house companies with guest appearances by visiting international orchestras and choirs. Most of the larger events are staged at the Teatro Comunale, which also serves as the festival's main box office (you are advised to reserve early), or at the Teatro Piccolo (or Ridotto), the Comunale's smaller auditorium. Other popular venues for smaller works include the Teatro della Pergola (see Classical Music for details), the Palazzo dei Congressi (see Classical Music for details), Teatro Verdi and Giardino dei Boboli. Information call (free-phone in Italy 199 112 112 www.maggioforentino.com).

Estate Fiesolana

The city's other big music festival is the Estate Fiesolana, a summer season of concerts held between late June and August. Like the Maggio Musicale it also offers peripheral opera, ballet, theatre and film presentations. Many of the concerts take place in attractive Fiesole in the hills above the city, where the old Teatro Romano (Roman theatre) provides a striking and escapist venue for a series of outdoor evening recitals. Other performances take place in the Badia Fiesolana nearby, or in Florence at a number of different locations such as Santa Croce and Palazzo Pitti.

Estate Fiesolana (Box Office)
✉ Piazza del Mercato 5
☎ 055/597 8308 or 597 044;
www.estatefiesole.it

Palazzo dei Congressi
✉ Viale F Strozzi (north of the rail station) ☎ No phone

Teatro Comunale
✉ Corso Italia 16, off Lungarno Amerigo Vespucci ☎ 055/277 9236 🚌 Shuttle bus C

Teatro della Pergola
✉ Via della Pergola 18, off Via Sant'Egidio ☎ 055/226 4333
🚌 6, 12, 14, 23, 71

Teatro Verdi
✉ Via Ghibellina 99
☎ 055/239 6242 🚌 14

Theatre

Virtually all of the Florentine theatrical productions staged will be beyond anyone without a good grasp of Italian. Bu if you do want to see a production, the city's leading theatres are the Teatro della Pergola with mainstream classical plays performed by leading Italian companies; the similar Teatro Verdi (see opposite); and for something quite different the Teatro Niccolini, one of the city's oldest theatres, offers a good mixture of classic modern and contemporary works.

Teatro Niccolini
✉ Via Ricasoli 3
☎ 055/213 282

Tuscany

Classical Music

Accademia Musicale Chigiana

Tuscany in the summer offers a wealth of small-town cultural festivals. One of the most prestigious belongs to Siena, where the Settimana Musicale Senese in July sees a week of performances by the acclaimed Accademia Musicale Chigiana.

✉ Via di Città 89, Siena
☎ 0577/22091;
www.chigiana.it   🕒 Jul

Festival Pucciniano

Equally well-known is the Festival Pucciniano, a series of outdoor concerts of Puccini's music held in August at Torre del Lago (near Lucca). Lucca itself stages the major Sagra Musicale Lucchese, a wide-ranging summer arts festival.

✉ Fondazione Festival Pucciniano, Torre del Lago
☎ Information: 0584/350 567.
Box office: 0584/359 322;
www.puccinifestival.it   🕒 Aug

Cantiere Internazionale d'Arte

Montepulciano's Cantiere Internazionale d'Arte (August) concentrates on new or more avante-garde works by composers, dramatists and choreographers. If you are unable to attend these larger festivals, enquire at tourist offices or keep your eyes open for posters advertising small church or other year-round recitals.

✉ Montepulciano
☎ 0578/757 089   🕒 Aug

San Gimignano

Slightly less exalted than the Festival Pucciniano or the Settimana Musicale Senese, but more varied and intimate, is the San Gimignano festival (in July), which has been held in the village virtually every year since the 1920s. It offers a wide range of music, film and theatrical presentations, usually culminating in two gala opera performances outdoors in the Piazza del Duomo. As with many of the festivals, reserve early (ideally before starting your holiday) to avoid disappointment.

✉ Piazza del Duomo 1
☎ 0577/940 008   🕒 Jul

Clubs and Discos

Nightlife of the clubs and disco variety, whether for teenagers or a sophisticated older crowd, is in very short supply in most of Tuscany's somnolent little hill towns. Exceptions include Siena, where there are a few clubs (situated mostly in the suburbs of the city), and occasional discos in and around Lucca, Pisa and Colle di Val d'Elsa (see up-to-date listings in *La Nazione*, Tuscany's local newspaper, for further details and locations).

There are also plenty of bars and clubs along the Versilia coast (north of Lucca), whose string of beach resorts play host to thousands of young summer visitors in search of night-time action. One of the most popular towns is Viareggio, thanks mainly to the fact it can be easily reached from Florence in around an hour. Many Florentines spend their summer nights in the town's many bars, nightclubs and seafood restaurants.

Another more upscale town with plenty of nightlife is Forte dei Marmi.

Something Different in Siena

The bi-annual bareback horse race around the Piazza del Campo is unmissable if the timing of your visit coincides with the Palio (➤ panel 116).

What's On When

The Palio

The most famous event in the Tuscan year is the Palio, a bi-annual bareback horse race (held in July and August) around the Piazza del Campo in Siena. Run virtually every year since medieval times, it takes its name from the *pallium*, or banner, awarded to the winner. Contestants are drawn from each of Siena's 17 contrade, or parishes, though only ten are represented in the race (lots are drawn to choose the ten). Competition is fierce—the race is far more than a tourist spectacle—as loyalty to the contrade is intense. Each has its own flag, heraldic motif (usually animal), as well as its own church, museum and social centre. Drummers and flag-tossers from each also parade in the orgy of processions and ceremonies that precede each Palio. The race lasts only 90 seconds, but celebrations can go on for weeks. If you can't be in Siena on race day, national television usually broadcasts the event live.

January

Pitti Immagine: Florence fashion shows.

February

Carnival celebrations across Tuscany, notably processions in Viareggio and San Gimignano (Shrove Tuesday and adjacent weekends).

March

Festa dell'Annunziata: fair in Florence's Piazza Santissima Annunziata (25th).

April

Lucca's summer Sagra Musicale (Music Festival) begins.
Holy Week celebrations many towns and villages
Mostra dell'Artigianato (Florence): international exhibition of crafts and artisans' work (last week).
Scoppo del Carro (Explosion of the Cart): Easter Sunday service in Florence's Duomo followed by special fireworks.

May

Festa del Grillo: crickets are sold and released in Florence's Cascine park (Sun after Ascension).
Maggio Musicale (Florence): international festival of music and dance.
Pisa's 'Historic Regatta of the Maritime Republics' (May–end Jun).

June

Start of summer arts and music festival in San Gimignano.
Luminaria di San Ranieri: fireworks and illuminated streets in Pisa followed the next day by a historic regatta.
Calcio in Costume: medieval soccer match in Florence *Il Gioco del Ponte*: Pisa's costumed 'Battle of the Bridge' (last Sun).
Estate Fiesolana: arts and musical festival in Fiesole.

July

Corso del Palio: world-famous horse race in Siena's main square (2nd).
Festa di San Paolino (Lucca): crossbow contest and procession.
Opera festival at Barga near Lucca (second half).

August

Cantiere Internazionale (Montepulciano): festival of contemporary music and dance (first half).
Montepulciano food festival (second Sun).
Corso del Palio: second horse race in Siena's main square (16th).
Luminaria di Santa Croce (Lucca): torchlit procession
Bravio delle Botti. (Montepulciano): barrel-rolling contest through the streets (last Sun).
International festival of choral music in Arezzo (last two weeks).
Festival Pucciniano: month-long outdoor festival of Puccini's music at Torre del Lago (near Lucca).
Settimana Musicale Senese: week-long music festival in Siena (last week).

September

Festa delle Rificolone (Florence): torchlit procession
Giostra del Saracino (Arezzo): jousting contest in medieval costume (first Sun).
Wine festivals across the region, notably Greve.

October

Florence opera and classical music season, the Teatro Comunale.

Practical Matters

Above: *Florentine marbled paper*
Right: Carabinieri, *Piazza della Signoria*

BEFORE YOU GO

WHAT YOU NEED

● Required
○ Suggested
▲ Not required

Some countries require a passport to remain valid for a minimum period (usually at least six months) beyond the date of entry—contact their consulate or embassy or your travel agent for details.

	UK	Germany	USA	Netherlands	Spain
Passport or National Identity Card where applicable	●	●	●	●	●
Visa (regulations can change—check before booking your trip)	▲	▲	▲	▲	▲
Onward or Return Ticket	▲	▲	▲	▲	▲
Health Inoculations	▲	▲	▲	▲	▲
Health Documentation (➤ 123, Health)	●	●	▲	●	●
Travel Insurance	○	○	○	○	○
Driving Licence (national)	●	●	●	●	●
Car Insurance Certificate (if own car)	○	○	○	○	○
Car Registration Document (if own car)	●	●	●	●	●

WHEN TO GO

Florence

High season / Low season

	JAN	FEB	MAR	APR	MAY	JUN	JUL	AUG	SEP	OCT	NOV	DEC
Season	Low	Low	Low	Low	High	High	High	High	High	Low	Low	Low
Temperature	6°C	6°C	10°C	13°C	17°C	22°C	25°C	25°C	21°C	16°C	11°C	6°C
Weather	Cloud	Cloud	Cloud	Wet	Sun	Sun	Sun	Sun	Sun	Wet	Very wet	Wet

Very wet · Wet · Cloud · Sun

TOURIST OFFICES

In the UK
Italian State Tourist Board
1 Princes Street
London W1R 8AY
☎ 020 7408 1254
Fax: 020 7493 6695
www.italiantouristboard.co.uk; www.enit.it

In the USA
Italian Government Travel Office (ENIT)
630 Fifth Avenue
Suite 1565,
Rockefeller Center
New York NY 10111
☎ 212/245 4822
Fax: 212/586 9249

Italian Government Travel Office (ENIT)
12400 Wilshire Boulevard
Suite 550
Los Angeles, CA 90025
☎ 310/820 1898
Fax: 310/820 6357

ARRIVING

The main entry into Tuscany is Pisa (Galileo Galilei) Airport (☎ 050/500 707; www.pisa-airport.com), though flights serve Perétola, close to Florence (☎ 055/315 874; www.safnet.it). There is a direct rail link between Florence and Pisa Airport (journey time 1 hour).

Pisa (Galileo Galilei) Airport
Kilometres to Pisa   **Journey times**

2 kilometres (1.25 miles)

🚇 5 minutes
🚌 4 minutes
🚗 10 minutes

Florence Perétola (Amerigo Vespucci) Airport
Kilometres to Florence   **Journey times**

5 kilometres (3 miles)

🚇 N/A
🚌 10 minutes
🚗 30 minutes

MONEY

The euro (€) is the official currency of Italy. Euro banknotes and coins were introduced in January 2002. Banknotes are issued in denominations of 5, 10, 20, 50, 100, 200 and 500 euros; coins in denominations of 1, 2, 5, 10, 20 and 50 cents, and 1 and 2 euros.

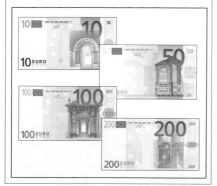

TIME

Italy is one hour ahead of Greenwich Mean Time (GMT+1), but from late March, when clocks are put forward one hour, to late September, Italian Summer Time (GMT+2) operates.

CUSTOMS

YES
From another EU country for personal use (guidelines)
800 cigarettes, 200 cigars, 1 kilogram of tobacco
10 litres of spirits (over 22%)
20 litres of aperitifs
90 litres of wine, of which 60 litres can be sparkling wine
110 litres of beer

From a non-EU country for your personal use, the allowances are:
200 cigarettes OR
50 cigars OR 250g of tobacco
1 litre of spirits (over 22%) 2 litres of intermediary products (eg sherry) and sparkling wine
2 litres of still wine
50g of perfume
0.25 litres of eau de toilette
The value limit for goods is 175 euros

Travellers under 17 years of age are not entitled to the tobacco and alcohol allowances.

NO
Drugs, firearms, ammunition, offensive weapons, obscene material, unlicensed animals.

TOURIST OFFICES

Florence Tourist Offices

- Via Cavour 1r
  Firenze (Florence)
  ☎ 055/290 832;
  www.firenzeturismo.it

- Borgo Santa Croce 29r
  Firenze (Florence)
  ☎ 055/234 0444

- Piazza della Stazione 4/A
  Firenze (Florence)
  ☎ 055/212 245

Other Tourist Offices

- Piazza della Repubblica 28
  Arezzo ☎ 0575/377 678

- Via Nazionale 42
  Visitors & Convention
  Cortona ☎ 0575/630 352

- Piazzale Giuseppe Verdi
  Lucca ☎ 0583/442 944

- Piazza del Duomo 1
  Pisa ☎ 050/560 464

- Piazza del Duomo 4
  Pistoia ☎ 0573/21 622

- Piazza del Duomo
  San Gimignano
  ☎ 0577/940 008

- Piazza del Campo 56
  Siena ☎ 0577/280 551

- Viale G Carducci 10
  Viareggio ☎ 0584/962 233

NATIONAL HOLIDAYS

J	F	M	A	M	J	J	A	S	O	N	D
2		1	2	1			1			1	4

1 Jan	New Year's Day
6 Jan	Epiphany
Mar/Apr	Easter Sunday and Monday
25 Apr	Liberation Day, 1945
1 May	Labour Day
15 Aug	Assumption of the Virgin
1 Nov	All Saints' Day
8 Dec	Immaculate Conception
25 Dec	Christmas Day
26 Dec	St. Stephen's Day
25 Dec	Christmas Day

Banks, businesses and most shops and museums are closed on these days. Florence celebrates its patron saint (St. John the Baptist) on 24 June, but most places stay open.

OPENING HOURS

○ Shops	● Attractions/museums
● Offices	● Post offices
● Banks	● Pharmacies

9am	10am	11am	12pm	2pm	3pm	4pm	5pm	6v

☐ Day	☐ Mid day
☐ Evening	

In addition to the times shown above, afternoon opening times of shops in winter is 3 to 6pm. Department stores and shops in tourist areas may remain open all day and sometimes, until later in the evening. Some shops are closed Monday morning, others on Saturday afternoon or all day Saturday. Nearly all shops close Sunday. Bank afternoon opening times vary but all are closed weekends. Museum times also vary—smaller museums tend to open only in the morning (9am to 1/2pm) and have restricted winter hours. Museums often close early on Sunday (around noon) and most close Monday.

PUBLIC TRANSPORT

Internal Flights Services throughout the country are provided by Alitalia—the national airline (☎ 06/65 621 or 65 643; www.alitalia.it) and smaller companies such as Meridiana, which flies to Perétola airport. Flights to Florence from Rome are 75 minutes; Milan 60

Trains Italian State Railways (Trenitalia; www.trenitalia.it) provides a well-run and inexpensive service. Florence is the hub of the Tuscan rail network with good connections with Pisa, Arezzo, Lucca and Viaréggio. The train is more comfortable than a bus but less frequent. There are two classes of travel: first and second.

Regional Buses There is no national bus company, though Lazzi (☎ 055/351 061; www.lazzi.it) and SITA (☎ 055/294 955; www.sita-on-line.it) both have a major presence in Tuscany. Bus terminals in larger towns are often next to the rail station; in smaller towns and villages most buses pull in at the central piazza.

Ferries Tuscany has three main ferry ports: Livorno serves Corsica, Sardinia, Sicily and the Tuscan Archipelago. Piombino has services to Elba, connecting to Portoferraio and Corsica, plus the smaller ports of Cavo and Rio Marina. Porto Santo Stefano has ferries to Corsica and the island of Giglio.

Urban Transport City buses are inexpensive charging a flat fare. Invariably you need a ticket before getting on. Buy them in tabacchi or from kiosks at bus terminals and stops. In Florence most routes pass by the station. Validate tickets on boarding. The service is reasonably frequent, but buses can get very crowded in rush hours.

CAR RENTAL

Car rental is available in most cities and resorts from international and Italian companies but is expensive. Generally small local firms offer better rates but cars can only be reserved locally. Air or train travellers can take advantage of special inclusive deals.

TAXIS

Taxis are available in all towns and tourist resorts. Taxis can be hailed, though you will be lucky to find one passing when you want one. Otherwise find a taxi rank (usually at stations and major piazze), or call a radio taxi (in Florence, ☎ 055/4390 or 055/4798).

DRIVING

Speed limits on the toll-operated motorways (autostrade): **130kph/80mph**

Speed limits on main roads: **110kph/68mph**; secondary roads: **90kph (55mph)**

Speed limits on urban roads: **50kph/31mph**

Must be worn in front seats at all times and in rear seats where fitted.

Random breath-testing. Never drive under the influence of alcohol.

Fuel is more expensive in Italy than in Britain and most other European countries, but diesel tends to be slightly less expensive. All except garages in rural places sell unleaded petrol (*senza piombo*). Outside urban areas petrol stations usually open 7am to 12.30pm and 3 to 7.30pm. Credit cards are rarely accepted.

In the event of a breakdown, ring 116, giving your registration number and type of car and the nearest ACI (Automobile Club d'Italia) office will assist you. You will be towed to the nearest ACI garage. This service is free to foreign-registered vehicles or cars rented from Rome or Milan airport (you will need to produce your passport).

PERSONAL SAFETY

The *Carabinieri* (military-style) uniforms and white shoulder belts) deal with general crime and public order. Tuscans are law-abiding. Petty theft is the main problem (bag-snatching, pickpocketing and car break-ins). Some precautions:
- Carry shoulder bags not *on* your shoulder but slung *across* your body.
- Scooter-borne bag-snatchers can be foiled if you keep well away from the edge of the road.
- Do not put anything down on a café or restaurant table.
- Lock car doors and never keep valuables in your car.

Police assistance:
☎ **112**
from any call box

TELEPHONES

Almost every bar in Italy has a telephone, plus many in public places. Tokens and phonecards are available from Telecom Italia offices, tobacconists, stations and other public places.

International Dialling Codes	
From Italy to:	
UK:	**00 44**
Germany:	**00 49**
USA:	**00 1**
Netherlands:	**00 31**
Spain:	**00 34**

POST

Post Offices
The Italian postal system can be notoriously slow. In Florence the central post office is at Via Pellicceria 8. Post offices in cities and major towns open 8am to 6pm (12.30pm Sat), other offices:
🕐 Mon–Fri 8.15–6, Sat 8.15–12pm. Closed Sun
☎ 055/214 145; www.poste.it

ELECTRICITY

The power supply is: 220 volts

Type of socket: Round two- or three-hole sockets taking plugs of two round pins or sometimes three pins in a vertical row. British visitors should bring an adaptor; US visitors a voltage transformer.

TIPS/GRATUITIES

Yes ✓ No ✗		
Hotels (if service not included)	✓	10–15%
Restaurants (if service not included)	✓	10–15%
Cafés/Bars	✓	€1 minimum
Taxis	✓	15%
Porters	✓	€1
Chambermaids	✓	€2 weekly
Usherettes	✓	10 cents
Hairdressers	✓	€2
Cloakroom attendants	✓	€1
Toilets	✓	10 cents min

HEALTH

Insurance
Nationals of EU countries receive medical treatment at reduced cost and pay a percentage of prescribed medicines. Hospital treatment is at reduced cost. You need a qualifying document (Form E111 for Britons). However, private medical insurance is advised for all.

Dental Services
Nationals of EU countries can obtain dental treatment at reduced cost at dentists who operate within the Italian health service. A qualifying document (Form E111 for Britons) is needed. Still, private medical insurance is advised for all.

Sun Advice
In summer, particularly in July and August, it can get very hot on the coast and low-lying land. You can get sunburnt surprisingly quickly, even through cloud, so a sunscreen is recommended at all times.

Drugs
Pharmacies (*farmacia*), recognized by their green cross sign, possess highly trained staff able to offer medical advice on minor ailments and provide a wide range of prescribed and non-prescribed medicines and drugs.

Safe Water
It is quite safe to drink tap water and water from drinking fountains, but never drink from a tap marked *acqua non potabile*. However, many Italians prefer the taste of bottled mineral, which is widely available.

CONCESSIONS

Students/Youths Holders of an International Student Identity Card (ISIC) can take advantage of discounts offered to travelling students. Those under 26 that are not students can obtain an International Youth Card from student organizations that entitles the holder to discounts on transport, accommodation, museums.

Senior Citizens Citizens aged over 60 (and under 18) of EU and a number of other countries with which Italy has a reciprocal arrangement (not including USA) may gain free admission to communal and state museums and receive discounts at other museums and on public transport on production of their passport.

CLOTHING SIZES

Italy	UK	Rest of Europe		
46	36	46	36	
48	38	48	38	
50	40	50	40	Suits
52	42	52	42	
54	44	54	44	
56	46	56	46	
41	7	41	8	
42	7.5	42	8.5	
43	8.5	43	9.5	Shoes
44	9.5	44	10.5	
45	10.5	45	11.5	
46	11	46	12	
37	14.5	37	14.5	
38	15	38	15	
39/40	15.5	39/40	15.5	Shirts
41	16	41	16	
42	16.5	42	16.5	
43	17	43	17	
38	8	34	6	
40	10	36	8	
42	12	38	10	Dresses
44	14	40	12	
46	16	42	14	
48	18	44	16	
38	4.5	38	6	
38	5	38	6.5	
39	5.5	39	7	Shoes
39	6	39	7.5	
40	6.5	40	8	
41	7	41	8.5	

LANGUAGE

Italian is the native language. The Tuscan dialect is the purest form of spoken Italian. Many Italians speak English, but you will be better received if you at least attempt to communicate in Italian. Italian words are pronounced phonetically. Every vowel and consonant (except 'h') is sounded. The accent usually (but not always) falls on the penultimate syllable.

Below is a list of a few words that may be helpful. More extensive coverage can be found in the AA's *Essential Italian Phrase Book* which lists 2,000 phrases and 2,000 words.

	English	Italian	English	Italian
	hotel	*albergo*	toilet	*toilette*
	room	*camera*	bath	*vasca*
	..single/double	*..singola/doppia*	shower	*doccia*
	..one/two nights	*..per una/due notte/i*	balcony	*balcone*
	..per person/per room	*..per una/due persona/e*	reception	*reception*
			key	*chiave*
	reservation	*prenotazione*	room service	*servizio da camera*
	rate	*tariffa*		
	breakfast	*prima colazione*	chambermaid	*cameriera*

	English	Italian	English	Italian
	bank	*banco*	banknote	*banconota*
	exchange office	*cambio*	coin	*moneta*
	post office	*posta*	credit card	*carta di credito*
	cashier	*cassiere/a*	traveller's cheque	*assegno turistico*
	foreign exchange	*cambio con l'estero*	commission charge	*commissione*
	foreign currency	*valuta estera*	cheque book	*libretto degli assegni*
	pound sterling	*sterlina*		
	American dollar	*dollaro*	exchange rate	*tasso di cambio*

	English	Italian	English	Italian
	restaurant	*ristorante*	starter	*il primo*
	café	*caffè*	main course	*il secondo*
	table	*tavolo*	dish of the day	*piatto del giorno*
	menu	*menù/carta*	dessert	*dolci*
	set menu	*menù turistico*	drink	*bevanda*
	wine list	*lista dei vini*	waiter	*cameriere*
	lunch	*pranzo/colazione*	waitress	*cameriera*
	dinner	*cena*	the bill	*conto*

	English	Italian	English	Italian
	aeroplane	*aeroplano*	..single/return	*..andata sola/andata e ritorno*
	airport	*aeroporto*		
	train	*treno*		
	..station	*stazione ferroviaria*	..first/second class	*..prima/seconda classe*
	bus	*autobus*	ticket office	*biglietteria*
	..station	*autostazione*	timetable	*orario*
	ferry	*traghetto*	seat	*posto*
	..terminal	*stazione maríttima*	non-smoking	*vietato fumare*
	ticket	*biglietto*	reserved	*prenotato*

	English	Italian	English	Italian
	yes	*sì*	help!	*aiuto!*
	no	*no*	today	*oggi*
	please	*per favore*	tomorrow	*domani*
	thank you	*grazie*	yesterday	*ieri*
	hello	*ciao*	how much?	*quanto?*
	goodbye	*arrivederci*	expensive	*caro*
	goodnight	*buona notte*	open	*aperto*
	sorry	*mi dispiace*	closed	*chiuso*

INDEX

Acknowledgements
The Automobile Association wishes to thank the following libraries, photographers and associations for their assistance in the preparation of this book:

THE BRIDGEMAN ART LIBRARY, LONDON 34b general view of the Chapel by Masolino and Filippino Lippi Masaccio (15th c.) Brancacci Chapel, Santa Maria del Carmine, Florence; 35b Battle of the Centaurs, relief by Michelangelo Buonarroti (1475–1564) (marble) Casa Buonarroti, Florence; 49b Pitti Palace: Vault of the Sala di Giove, paintings by Pietro da Cortona and Ciro Ferri, 1643
SCALA 38b Giardino di Boboli, Florence
SPECTRUM COLOUR LIBRARY 61
www.euro.ecb.int/ 119 (euro notes).

The remaining pictures are from the Association's own library (AA PHOTO LIBRARY) and were taken by C Sawyer with the exception of the following: J Edmanson 5b, 11b, 40b, 46b, 50, 55b, 86, 122c; K Paterson 1, 2, 6b, 7b, 9b, 10b, 12b, 19b, 21, 22b, 27a, 43b, 59b, 67, 70a, 71, 72a, 72b, 73a, 74a, 75, 76a, 77, 78, 79a, 79b, 80, 80/1, 82, 83a, 83b, 84, 85a, 88, 89, 90, 91b, 117b; B Smith 27b, 31b, 54/5, 62b, 91a, 92, 93, 94, 95, 96, 97, 98, 99, 100, 101, 102, 103, 104, 105, 106, 107, 108, 109, 110, 111, 112, 113, 114, 115, 116, 122a; T Souter 56b; W Voysey 117a.

Author's Acknowledgements Tim Jepson wishes to thank his editor and Duncan and Amanda Baird.

Contributors
Managing Editors: Apostrophe S Limited Page Layout: Design 23
Researcher (Practical Matters): Colin Follett Indexer: Marie Lorimer

Dear Essential Traveller

Your comments, opinions and recommendations are very important to us. So please help us to improve our travel guides by taking a few minutes to complete this simple questionnaire.

You do not need a stamp (unless posted outside the UK). If you do not want to cut this page from your guide, then photocopy it or write your answers on a plain sheet of paper.

Send to: **The Editor, AA World Travel Guides, FREEPOST SCE 4598, Basingstoke RG21 4GY.**

Your recommendations...

We always encourage readers' recommendations for restaurants, nightlife or shopping – if your recommendation is used in the next edition of the guide, we will send you a *FREE* AA *Essential* Guide of your choice. Please state below the establishment name, location and your reasons for recommending it.

_____
_____
_____
_____

Please send me **AA *Essential*** _____

About this guide...

Which title did you buy?
    AA *Essential* _____
Where did you buy it? _____
When? m m / y y

Why did you choose an AA *Essential* Guide? _____

_____
_____
_____
_____

Did this guide meet your expectations?
    Exceeded ☐ Met all ☐ Met most ☐ Fell below ☐
    Please give your reasons _____

_____
_____
_____

continued on next page...

Were there any aspects of this guide that you particularly liked? _____

_____

_____

Is there anything we could have done better? _____

_____

_____

About you...

Name (*Mr/Mrs/Ms*) _____

Address _____

_____

_____ Postcode _____

Daytime tel nos _____

Please only give us your mobile phone number if you wish to hear from us
about other products and services from the AA and partners by text or mms.

Which age group are you in?
   Under 25 ☐   25–34 ☐   35–44 ☐   45–54 ☐   55–64 ☐   65+ ☐

How many trips do you make a year?
   Less than one ☐   One ☐   Two ☐   Three or more ☐

Are you an AA member? Yes ☐   No ☐

About your trip...

When did you book? m m / y y   When did you travel? m m / y y
How long did you stay? _____
Was it for business or leisure? _____
Did you buy any other travel guides for your trip?
   If yes, which ones? _____

Thank you for taking the time to complete this questionnaire. Please send it to us as soon as
possible, and remember, you do not need a stamp (*unless posted outside the UK*).

Happy Holidays!